The Promises to the Fathers

Claus Westermann

THE PROMISES
TO THE FATHERS

Studies on the Patriarchal Narratives

translated by
DAVID E. GREEN

FORTRESS PRESS   PHILADELPHIA

Translated by David E. Green from the German *Die Verheissungen an die Väter* © 1976 Vandenhoeck & Ruprecht, Göttingen.

Library of Congress Cataloging in Publication Data

Westermann, Claus.
   The promises to the fathers.

   Translation of Die Verheissungen an die Väter.
   Includes bibliographical references and index.
   1. Bible. O.T. Genesis—Criticism, interpretation, etc. 2. Patriarchs (Bible) I. Title.
BS1235.2.W45413   222′.11′06   79-7395
ISBN 0-8006-0580-2

7689D79   Printed in the United States of America   1–580

Dedicated to
The Society for Old Testament Study
in England
in gratitude for being made
an honorary member

Contents

Abbreviations

BASOR   Bulletin of the American Schools of Oriental Research

BWANT   Beiträge zur Wissenschaft vom Alten und Neuen Testament

BZAW   Beihefte zur Zeitschrift für die Alttestamentlich Wissenschaft

HAT   Handbuch zum Alten Testament

NF   Neue Folge

ZAW   Zeitschrift für die Alttestamentliche Wissenschaft

Foreword

My study "Types of Narrative in Genesis," published in German
by Kaiser-Verlag in 1964 in *Forschung am Alten Testament* as
Volume 24 of the Theologische Bücherei series, dealt with the
promises to the patriarchs and the narratives containing these
promises. The approaches sketched out there needed to be followed up, which I have attempted to do in the present work.
Since the latter refers in many places to the earlier study and presupposes it, it is reprinted here as Part A; the 1964 publication is
out of print. No changes have been made except for minor cor-
rections. I wish to express my thanks to the Kaiser-Verlag for
permission to reprint this material.

Parts B ("The Promises to the Fathers," minus section I) and
C ("The Significance of the Ugaritic Texts for the Patriarchal
Narratives") were delivered with minor changes as lectures before the Spanish Exegetical Society at Bilbao in April, 1974. I am
grateful to my Spanish colleagues for a stimulating time together.

The notes to Part C, the Ugaritic parallels, were produced by
Dr. K. Günther of the Center for Ugaritic Studies at Heidelberg,
to whom I wish to take this opportunity to express my thanks.

C. WESTERMANN

The Promises to the Fathers

Types of Narrative in Genesis
(1964)

Introduction

In the interpretation of the Genesis narratives, there are today two absolutely contrary approaches or methodologies, between which there can be hardly any agreement granted the present state of scholarship. On the one hand, we have the approach deriving from Gunkel's commentary on Genesis (especially the principles laid down in the introduction); in this line of development, as exemplified by Noth's *A History of Pentateuchal Traditions* and von Rad's *Genesis*, the dominant question is the history of traditions. On the other, we have the American school, especially that of Albright and his students, characterized by heavy use of archaeology; these scholars emphasize the historicity of the patriarchs and the patriarchal narratives and thus consider it possible to reconstruct the period of the patriarchs, as can be seen in several accounts bearing the title "The Patriarchal Age." A good and particularly pregnant example is the third chapter, "The Founding Fathers," of G. Ernest Wright's *Biblical Archaeology* (1957).

The one side tends to accept the Genesis narratives as directly as possible as accounts of events that took place just as described, preserved by an uninterrupted tradition. The other side tends to emphasize the work of writers and narrators throughout the historical period of Israel in shaping stories that were much earlier, asking about the course of tradition taken by these narratives *within Israel*. To them, the question of what the narratives can still tell us about the patriarchal period itself appears very difficult or even impossible to answer.

The following study is an attempt to advance a step beyond this antithesis by inquiring into the nature of these narratives, which, deriving from preliterary strata, contain material from the prehistoric period that we still might recognize.

I

Promise Narratives

THE PROMISE MOTIF IN MODERN STUDY

The promise motif in the patriarchal narratives has been heavily emphasized by recent scholars such as Noth, von Rad, and Zimmerli. In every instance this emphasis has derived from examination of the patriarchal history as a whole within the larger context of the Pentateuch or Hexateuch, within which it is such an important and significant element. Examples include §7c, "The Theme 'Promise to the Patriarchs,' " in Martin Noth's *A History of Pentateuchal Traditions* (trans. B. W. Anderson [Englewood Cliffs, N. J.: Prentice-Hall, 1972], pp. 54–58) and Gerhard von Rad's statement in Volume 1 of his *Old Testament Theology* (trans. D. M. G. Stalker [New York: Harper, 1962]) in the introduction to the section on the history of the patriarchs (p. 167).

> Although the great narrative complexes covering the call of Abraham down to the death of Joseph consist in the coalescence

2

of a great variety of traditional material, the whole has nevertheless a scaffolding supporting and connecting it, the so-called promise to the patriarchs. At least it can be said that this whole variegated mosaic of stories is given cohesion of subject-matter . . . by means of the constantly recurring divine promise.

Therefore the picture of the patriarchal stories here differs so greatly from that which results from Gunkel's introduction to his commentary on Genesis. Since Gunkel puts most emphasis on the individual narrative and within each narrative takes the smallest unit as his starting point, the thematic importance of the promise for the patriarchal narratives, making them a coherent whole, was beyond his purview.

This situation, however, necessarily raises a question: what is the relationship of this element of the promise, so important for the patriarchal narratives as a whole, to the individual narratives? Is it possible to say that the promise to the patriarchs is the basic element of many individual narratives in Genesis? In other words, is it possible to recognize in the narratives of Genesis a literary type or genre of "promise narrative"?

This question was examined by J. Hoftijzer in his study *Die Verheissungen an die drei Erzväter* (Leiden: Brill, 1956); he arrived at the conclusion that in the two groups of promises that he distinguishes (in effect the P narratives and the JE narratives) only one of the narratives in each group has a promise originally associated with it, in the one case Genesis 15 (which he considers a unit) and in the other Genesis 17. In *all* other instances the promises did not originate contemporaneously with the narrative, but were appended to or inserted in the narrative later, as in Genesis 22. Whether or not Hoftijzer's conclusion is accepted (a point to which I shall return), it follows clearly that distinction must be drawn between the origin of the patriarchal narratives and their association with the promise motif. Each of the many narratives in which we find words of promise may have originated as a promise narrative, but need not have. At the same time, it must be stated at the outset that this distinction with the classi-

3

fication it produces differs from the literary distinction according to sources and their various redactions, which it precedes.[1]

In one point this distinction corresponds to one of Alt's hypotheses, which was developed further by Noth and von Rad, namely that the promise of the land at one time had a goal it can no longer have in the form of the patriarchal history that has come down to us. As von Rad puts it (*Theology*, vol. 1, p. 168): ". . . we have to bear in mind that the twofold promise, particularly that of the possession of the land as originally understood, had reference to an imminent and direct fulfilment, that of the settlement of the patriarchs in the land of Canaan." This hypothesis needs to be extended only a little: when the narratives of the promise of the land to the patriarchs lost their original goal, they also lost their true and original structure, and were therefore unable to survive as narratives once their immediate goal had vanished, namely the fulfillment of the promise to the patriarchs themselves during their lifetime or to their sons in their clan. We should not expect to find this ancient stratum of narratives promising the land to the patriarchs in the patriarchal history as transformed from the perspective of the Pentateuch as a whole, but only echoes or modifications, transformations associated with new elements.

This might be the case, for example, in the short independent passage Genesis 12:7.[2]

> And Yahweh appeared to Abraham
> and said, "To your descendants I will give this land."

---

1. For this reason, the discussion that follows touches only occasionally on the question of source analysis. In general, it can be said that for the question under discussion of the types of narrative in Genesis, there is a significant difference between P on the one hand and JE on the other. When P himself is telling the story, he has usually had a profound effect on the nature and form of the ancient narratives, transforming them thoroughly to correspond to his style and theology; JE, on the other hand, both tend to preserve the ancient narratives as intact as possible.

2. This verse is an independent unit (pace Gunkel, Procksch, von Rad, et. al.); it is preceded by the concluding statement "At that time the Canaanites were in the land," and is followed by what is itself an independent itinerary in verses 8–9.

So he built there an altar
to Yahweh, who had appeared to him.

Viewed from the perspective of narrative content, this is a coherent, self-contained event consisting of three elements. It can be imagined in the context of a narrative in which the element of tension would be generated by the relationship between the promise "I will give" and some corresponding exigency, necessity, or expectation. The elimination of this tension has transformed the narrative into a mere allusion to a narrative. In this case it is clear that the original tension has been replaced by a different tension, which is now expressed in the prologue, 12:1–3: the command to set out toward an unknown goal, "to the land that I will show you."

In this case, 12:7 would be an allusion to a narrative belonging to the earlier stratum in which the promise of the land and the gift of the land was still made to the clan of the patriarchs, not to Israel.

First, however, we must examine the question of what were originally promises or how the various promises relate to each other. Recent studies of the promise in the patriarchal stories exhibit an obvious uncertainty on this point.

The crucial new approach in the question of the significance of the promises appears in Albrecht Alt's study "The God of the Fathers." According to Alt,[3] the promise narratives in their present form were composed by the literary editors, J and E. But they contained accurate reminiscences of the patriarchal period in that the promises are ascribed regularly to the gods of patriarchs, not the 'ēlîm. The promise of the land could just as easily have been associated with the gods of the land. Alt goes a step further here in a careful consideration of the relationship between the two different promises:

The promises are concerned almost exclusively with two mat-

---

3. See especially Albrecht Alt, "The God of the Fathers," in his *Essays on Old Testament History and Religion* (Oxford: Blackwell, 1966), pp. 64ff.

ters, the increase of the patriarchs' posterity, and their possession of the Promised Land. Here again it almost seems as if two
separate sets of ideas have been combined, one originating before
the entry, and the other in Palestine itself. On the one hand
there is the concern of a nomadic tribe for the maintenance and
increase of its numbers, and on the other the claim of settlers
to own their land. But it is not men alone who have these aims
at heart, but also their god, who assures the earthly prosperity of
his worshippers.

Here the promise of posterity is clearly labeled earlier, associated with the nomadic period, while the promise of the land is
associated with the claims of "settlers." Alt bases this distinction
between the two promises on his interpretation of Genesis 15,
which is merely intimated:

> [I refer] to the story in Genesis xv, and to the question raised
> above, as to whether or not it goes back to an aetiological saga
> concerning the God of Abraham. . . . This makes it highly prob-
> able that it was the God of Abraham, especially since its earliest
> Yahwist form concludes with the simple promise of a son to
> Abraham. (Note: . . . I follow PROCKSCH in taking the references
> to the land Abraham is to possess in the future [Gen. xv. 7, 18b,
> 19–20] as later additions.) It would seem to be a genuinely an-
> cient passage, standing first in the series of revelations by the
> God of the Fathers, which the Yahwist continues through Isaac
> to Jacob, composing each account himself. We can probably
> think of all the cultic sagas of the gods of the Fathers as having
> a similar pattern.[4]

In Genesis 15, then, we may see what is still a pre-Palestinian
promise narrative, concluding "with the simple promise of a son
to Abraham." It comes at the beginning of a series of revelations
of the God of the patriarchs, extended freely by the Yahwist.

Noth takes Alt's conclusion as his point of departure, albeit
without distinguishing between the promises:

> What is essential concerning the origin and nature of the patri-
> archal tradition has been said by Albrecht Alt. . . . This type of

---

4. Alt, *Essays*, pp. 65–66.

cult . . . was characterized by a *personal* relationship of the deity to his worshipers. . . . This religion included above all the divine promise of the inheritance of the land and a numerous posterity. . . .[5]

For Noth, the theme "Promise to the Patriarchs" includes both the promise of posterity and the promise of the land from the very outset. If one of the two is stressed, it is the promise of the land (pp. 56, 81). But the relationship between the two is never felt to be a problem; for Noth there was clearly no question on this point. A difficulty arises, however, when Noth supports his thesis on the basis of Genesis 15, which he, like Alt, considers a fundamental passage for the promise to the patriarchs. While for Alt the Yahwistic nucleus of this narrative contains *only* the promise of a son for Abraham, for Noth the same narrative confirms the double promise.[6]

Like Noth, von Rad takes Alt's conclusions as his point of departure.[7] He cites Alt's study with special emphasis on the promise of the land (pp. 82–83).

> It was evidently the contribution of the Yahwist to fuse the whole complex of the patriarchal sagas together. . . . The question therefore arises, where did the Yahwist find this new element? How did he come to include the whole mass of patriarchal sagas within the scheme of the promise of land in this way? Alt has given us the answer in his book on the God of the patriarchs: it is because the promise of the land is an original element of the pre-Mosaic cultus of the God of the patriarchs. . . . The God of the patriarchs had already promised possession of the land to the ancestors of Israel when they lived in tents on the edge of the

5. M. Noth, *A History of Pentateuchal Traditions*, p. 55; see also pp. 56, 81, 102, 111.

6. A further difficulty will only be alluded to here. Noth assumes that all these promise narratives were originally associated with a specific locale. Here, too, he parts company with Alt, who assigns localization not to the earliest stratum but a later one. In the case of the God of the Fathers, a connection with a specific sanctuary plays no role at all; the important thing is the connection with one group of people (Alt, *Essays*, pp. 22–23).

7. G. von Rad, "The Promised Land and Yahweh's Land in the Hexateuch" in his *The Problem of the Hexateuch and Other Essays* (Edinburgh: Oliver & Boyd, 1966), pp. 79–93.

7

settled territory, a fact which is quite clearly shown by the saga which has come down from that time almost intact (Gen. xv.7ff.).

For the thesis that the promise of the land was an original element, von Rad, as we have seen, cannot cite Alt's support. Once again, this can be seen in the appeal to Genesis 15, which Alt interprets differently, maintaining that the references to future possession of the land in Genesis 15:7, 18b, 19 are later additions (see above). But von Rad adds a further argument. He inquires into the priority of the promises and comes to the conclusion: "The promise of land predominated decisively here." The same conclusion reappears in his Theology, Volume 1, pages 168–69, with the addition of a further important argument: "Deuteronomy, which very often appeals to the promise to the patriarchs, understood it only as a promise of the land." This raises the question of how this predominance is to be explained and how the limitation came about in Deuteronomy.

Zimmerli[8] takes as his point of departure the fact that the promise of the land was the original promise:

> The original content of the promise to the fathers may have consisted in the pledge of the land. . . . Very early, however, the pledge of a great posterity was ranked alongside it. . . . There is a sharp contrast between the fathers, on the one hand, singled out and separated from their clans, and, on the other hand, the existence of Israel in its fullness as a whole people. In humble, astonished confession, the biblical writers express this in the symbolic figures of the stars of the heavens, the sand of the sea, and the dust of the earth (pp. 91–92).

Thus Zimmerli inquires into "the original content of the promise to the fathers," but his answer is the opposite to Alt's answer to the same question. In addition, Zimmerli sees Genesis 12:1–3 in a different light than others before him. For him, the dominant theme in this prologue by the Yahwist is the concept of blessing:

8. W. Zimmerli, "Promise and Fulfillment," in Essays on Old Testament Hermeneutics, ed. C. Westermann (Richmond: John Knox, 1963), pp. 89–122.

[Genesis 12:1–3] indeed sounds the note of land and posterity as elements of promise, but it clearly places them in the shadow of the pledge of a blessing (unmistakable in the fivefold use of the root brk). "Blessing" here means more than a mere numerical increase (p. 92).

The state of the discussion today is summarized by Hoftijzer in his study (see above):

G. von Rad and M. Noth, following the lead of A. Alt. . . . On the basis of comparative material, there is good reason to state that there is an historical basis for a cult of the gods of the fathers. Alt concludes his book with the conjecture that the promise of posterity was the original content of the cults, and that the pledge of the land was added after the entrance into Canaan. Von Rad and Noth are basically in agreement. They do not, however, consider the promise of posterity to be the essential content of the patriarchal cults, but rather the promise of the land. . . . This interpretation means, among other things, that the promises to the patriarchs constituted from the very outset the nucleus of the traditions concerning the patriarchal period, and that all other traditions found a place within this framework (pp. 4–5).

In contrast to these scholars, Hoftijzer prefers to follow the methodology suggested by Stärk's essay "Studien zur Religions- und Sprachgeschichte des Alten Testaments" (1899), ". . . to the extent that we must first elucidate in every aspect of their present context the traditional forms that have been preserved before attempting to determine the historical sequences of the various strata of tradition." Hoftijzer is correct in insisting that for each of the promise texts we must first inquire into its relationship to the narrative in which we find it or with which it is associated. He is also right in asserting that in the overwhelming majority of the passages in which we find a promise made to one of the patriarchs, this promise represents a secondary addition or interpolation. Given these circumstances, it is by no means so simple to represent the promises as the fundamental element of the patriarchal narratives.

Hoftijzer's positive thesis, however, is itself problematic. We

9

have already noted that he finds only a single text in each of two groups of texts in which the promise is an original element of the narrative. These two are Genesis 15 and 17.

> Only in Genesis 15, which is to be understood as a single unit, is the promise of posterity and the land an original component of the narrative. . . . In a nocturnal vision Yahweh promises Abraham not only a son, but numerous descendants. Abraham believes the promise, incredible as it seems. As a reward (sic), Yahweh also gives him the promise of the land, confirmed, at Abraham's request, by a covenant ceremony.[9]

Once again, as in the case of Alt, Noth, and von Rad, Genesis 15 is the key passage. Hoftijzer considers the whole chapter a single unit. His argument that Yahweh adds the promise of the land because Abraham believes the promise of descendants is highly questionable. A promise as a reward for proper conduct is a late combination of two motifs that are essentially different. Similarly, Hoftijzer goes on to say, chapter 17 is the central text of the other group, the only independent narrative that contains both the promise of the land and the promise of many descendants. Here, too then, a different conclusion, based once again on a different exegesis of Genesis 15, is fundamental for the promise narratives.

So the entire question remains open. Was the promise of the land linked from the very outset with the promise of posterity? Or did they have different origins? The problem of what criteria to apply is obviously very obscure. Our survey shows clearly that it will simply not suffice to base a general hypothesis concerning the promise narratives on a single text. The obscurity of this crucial passage, however, practically demands investigation.

THE DISTRIBUTION OF THE DIFFERENT PROMISES

We shall first attempt to determine what possibilities the texts suggest for distributing the different promises. The discussion to this point appears to reckon with three possibilities:

9. *Verheissungen*, p. 23.

1) descendants alone
2) the land alone
3) the land and descendants together

But if all the relevant passages are examined, it is immediately clear that this does not exhaust all the possibilities. The promise of a son is not identical with the promise of descendants (that is, the promise of many descendants), but represents an independent type. It is developed most fully in Genesis 18, but is encountered elsewhere. In addition, there is what might be called a promise of blessing (recognized by Zimmerli in Gen. 12:1–3), or, put somewhat differently, a combination of a blessing with a promise in various forms, most fully developed in Genesis 12:1–3. Thus three additional possibilities must be added:

4) a son alone
5) descendants and a son
6) a blessing combined with various other promises

When we examine the texts in the light of these possibilities, we see at once that the combinations predominate. The only major group of texts embodying a single promise is the group recording the promise of the land. Once, in 18:10ff., we find the single promise of a son. This first survey of the distribution does not yield much, but one point is clear already: a survey certainly does not support the conclusion that from the very outset the promise to the patriarchs included both descendants and the land.

This survey suggests a further conclusion, namely that the promise of a son (or a child) is a separate, independent motif, in many cases linked secondarily with the promise of many descendants. We shall now pursue this motif.

THE PROMISE OF A SON

We have already noted that the fullest development of this motif is found in Genesis 18. In the narrative of the visit of the men to Abraham in 18:1–15, the promise of the *birth* of a child

11

is the climax of the story. The tension that is resolved in this promise (and its fulfillment) was engendered by Sarah's childlessness. Of any general promise of many descendants the narrative contains not a trace; it forms a complete and coherent whole without such a promise. The promise of a child (and the fulfillment of this promise) *totally* resolves the tension and *totally* solves the problem; there is no place within the scope of this incident for any promise of many descendants.

We may draw two conclusions: (1) in this narrative, the mere promise of a son is certainly the original element; and (2) the promise forms a necessary part of this narrative, which is based on the problem of childlessness, from the very outset, and is clearly an original element of this narrative. Genesis 18, then, is a true promise narrative (that is, a narrative involving a promise as a necessary element and from the very outset); but what is promised is neither the land nor a multitude of descendants, but a son. In other words, the narrative of Genesis 18 belongs in the realm of the family. It is essential to the nature of the promise in this narrative that the span between promise and fulfillment is as short as possible: "at this time next year . . . ." It stays within the lifetime of a generation.

THE PROMISE OF A SON AND MANY DESCENDANTS

In the other passages, the promise of a son is coupled with the promise of many descendants (the promise of increase). How is this combination to be understood in detail?

Genesis 16:1–16. In 16:10–12, the two promises stand juxtaposed without any link:

> The angel of Yahweh also said to her,
> "I will greatly multiply your descendants,
> that they cannot be numbered for multitude!"
> And the angel of Yahweh said to her,
> "Behold, you are with child and shall bear a son. . . ."

The introductions to the two promises are absolutely identical (10a = 11a). In verse 10, the formula introduces the promise of many descendants, in verse 11, the promise of the birth of a child. That these two promises did not originate together is shown not only by the repeated introduction but by the variation in form: verse 10b is prose, 11b poetry. The announcement of a child together with a prediction of his future is a frequently attested form (especially in the tribal sayings).[10] We can therefore safely say that the narrative in Genesis 16 originally contained only the promise of the birth of a son, and that the promise of many descendants was added when the story was included in the cycle of patriarchal or Abraham stories, in order to integrate them more firmly into this new context by use of a kind of leitmotif. It is certainly true in any case that the promise of a son is a necessary part of the Hagar narrative, but the promise of many descendants is not absolutely necessary. The difference is expressed in the loose way the second promise is appended, literarily and grammatically. Thus the Hagar narrative in the form of Genesis 16 is of the same type as Genesis 18. We then have two narratives in which (a) the promise of a son stands by itself and (b) is necessary to the narrative.

Genesis 21. In the other Hagar narrative the whole situation is different, because both Isaac and Ishmael are already born. The tension in this narrative is engendered by the danger that Hagar, banished by Abraham, will perish of thirst as she goes through the desert. The story is a preservation narrative: God saves the child of Hagar (and of Abraham) from dying of thirst, the same motif encountered in the preservation narratives surrounding Israel's desert wandering.

The beginning of the narratives cites the promise of a son that was given to Abraham (vv. 12–13):

---

10. The commentaries (for example, Eissfeldt's Hexateuch-Synopse and Gunkel's Genesis) account for the difficulty by means of redactional additions.

> Be not displeased because of the lad and because of your slave
> woman;
> whatever Sarah says to you, do as she tells you,
> for through Isaac shall your descendants be named.
> And I will make a nation of the son of the slave woman also,
> because he is your offspring.

This speech clearly has a synthesizing and linking function. It presupposes narratives already in being: the birth of the son of Sarah promised to Abraham and the birth of the son born to Abraham by Sarah's handmaid. It therefore does not belong to the stage of initial origin of the individual narratives, but to a later stage when they were linked together and combined to form a larger narrative cycle.[11] In addition, verse 13 shows that this recension of the Hagar narrative already presupposes that the promise of a son has been combined with the promise of many descendants. This is shown especially by the word "also," which presupposes that the allusion to the promise of a son (Isaac) was heard in connection with the promise of many descendants.

It is from this perspective also that the promise to Hagar in verses 17–18 must be understood:

> And God heard the voice of the lad; . . .
> "What troubles you, Hagar? Fear not;
> for God has heard the voice of the lad where he is.
> Arise, lift up the lad, and hold him fast with your hand;
> for I will make him a great nation.

When 18b uses exactly the same words that had previously been spoken to Abraham (v. 13), we may assume that we are dealing with a deliberate form of composition. The story tells how, *despite* the banishment of Hagar, Ishmael will also become a (great) nation, because he is Abraham's seed. This would mean that the Hagar narrative (21:8–21) as a whole belongs to the stage determined from verses 12–13. The preservation narrative has been combined so artfully with the motif of the promise of

---

11. The late origin of these verses is demonstrated at length by Gunkel in his commentary on verses 11–13.

14

many descendants that it appears to be all of a piece. The promise of many descendants cannot be isolated and removed (as in 16:10). It cannot be said, however, that the preservation narrative absolutely demands the promise of many descendants as its goal.

Genesis 15:1–6. What is the relationship between the promise of a son and the promise of many descendants in 15:1–6? The first thing we notice in this text is the striking prophetic formula in verse 1: *hāyāh d^ebar yhwh 'el 'abrām*, repeated in verse 4. This is a sure sign that the pericope received its final form in a period in which these prophetic formulas were being used as stylistic devices outside of prophecy proper. When we examine the structure of the passage (which is similar to vv. 7–21), we note several elements that are usually termed cultic.[12]

1a. Introduction: the word of Yahweh comes to Abraham.
1b. Pledge of salvation and prosperity.
2. Reply: statement of grievance.
3. Reply: statement of grievance.
4. God's answer:
   a) Future salvation: a consanguineous heir;
5. b) Confirming sign.
6. Conclusion: Abraham believed . . . .

This structure exhibits striking affinities to what Begrich calls an oracle of salvation, which is given in response to a complaint or lament and consists of a pledge of salvation ("Fear not!" followed by a perfect or noun clause) and (usually) an announcement of salvation in the future. That this structure can be used as the basis of a narrative is also shown by Judges 6, the story of Gideon, where we also find the addition of a sign confirming the announcement of salvation. This is not the place to discuss the origin and history of this structure. It suffices to state that the

---

12. O. Kaiser, "Traditionsgeschichtliche Untersuchung von Gen. 15," ZAW 70 (1958): 107–126. See H. Seebass, "Zu Genesis 15," *Wort und Dienst*, N.F. 7 (1963): 132–49.

structure shows itself to be essentially different from that of a simple narrative in that it presents something that takes place over and over again, in contrast to a simple narrative, which by nature recounts something unique. In Genesis 15:1ff., the structure is given in advance; quite apart from the story of Abraham, it was already extant in another domain (in the broad sense cultic or liturgical), from which it was taken to serve as a setting for the Abraham narrative.

When we examine the promise itself, the assurance of salvation in verse 1 turns out to be an already extant saying now applied to Abraham:

> After these things
> the word of Yahweh came to Abraham in a vision,
> "Fear not, Abram,
> I am your shield; your reward shall be very great."
> (Or: "I will make your reward very great.")

In other words, the promise given by God to Abraham has been couched in a form of language already existing in another domain. The form is probably that of the assurance of success and salvation addressed to a king.[13] In this usage, shield and reward are political concepts. "Reward" is used in exactly the same sense in Isaiah 40:1-11: "his reward is with him" (v. 10). They are therefore appropriate to a totally different way of life than that of Abraham.

When Abraham replies with a statement of his grievance, God responds with an announcement of salvation (future), consisting in the announcement of a consanguineous heir (v. 4):

> And behold, the word of Yahweh came to him,
> "This man shall not be your heir;
> your own son
> shall be your heir."

---

13. Kaiser, "Untersuchung von Gen. 15," p. 115: "We are dealing with what was originally an oracle of salvation addressed to a king, to whom the god promises protection in battle, victory, and rich booty." As a parallel, Kaiser cites an oracle addressed to Esarhaddon by Ishtar of Arbela: "Esarhaddon, in Arbela I am your gracious shield."

This is actually not formulated as a promise; the formulation derives rather from the statement of Abraham's grievance (v. 3):

> Behold, thou hast given me no offspring;
> and a slave born in my house will be my heir.

Here again a fixed form has replaced free narrative. Instead of a narrative description of the situation, namely Abraham's child-lessness, we have its reflex in a formal lament. From this fixed lament formula there then arises its opposite and thus the answer that announces salvation.

Verse 5 represents the confirming sign in the fixed structure. A sign confirming the promise is also alluded to in Genesis 18: "At the appointed time I will return to you. . . ." Here the sign refers explicitly to the birth of the child. In Genesis 15:5, on the contrary, the sign—to great effect!—consists in a new and different promise, the promise of many descendants. It is given the form of a sign through the context that introduces it:

> And he brought him outside and said,
> "Look toward heaven, and number the stars,
> if you are able to number them."

Here is used one of the frequent images associated with the promise of many descendants.

> 26:4 I will multiply your descendants as the stars of heaven.
> 32:12 I will make your descendants as the sand of the sea,
> which cannot be numbered for multitude.
> 16:10 I will so greatly multiply your descendants
> that they cannot be numbered for multitude.

One may well ask whether Genesis 15:5 is a poetic elaboration of the simple promise of many descendants. The reverse is also possible: that this formulation in Genesis 15:5 represents a kind of leveling of what was originally a poetic scene. But this is less likely.

Clear evidence to the contrary is the striking circumstance that in a preexisting structure the promise of a son serves as an announcement of salvation and the promise of many descendants

17

as a sign confirming the former promise. This suggests a secondary combination of the two promises in 15:1–6. But they have been combined so successfully that it would be equally possible to assume a narrative in which the promise of a son and of many descendants constituted a single unit in the original draft. What demands caution with respect to this hypothesis is the clearly identifiable structure of a salvation oracle, including elements that are alien to the patriarchal narrative: the prophetic introductions and the assurance of salvation in verse 1, which derives from the liturgical realm.

CONCLUSION: In Genesis 18 and 16 we are dealing with the promise of the birth of a son, without additional promise elements. Both pericopes belong to the genre of an original promise narrative, a narrative in which the birth of a son or child is promised. In chapter 16, the promise of many descendants has been loosely appended.

The composition of the Hagar narrative in chapter 21 presupposes the combination of the two promises. It leads up to the promise of many descendants (for Ishmael); this, however, is not the goal of a promise narrative but of a preservation narrative.

Genesis 15:1–6 is a promise narrative that has been cast in the form of a salvation oracle and reveals traces of language alien to the patriarchal narratives. Here the two promises probably constituted a single unit even in the first draft of the narrative; this unit, however, is not an original promise narrative but rather a combination presupposing the two promises together with other elements (see above). We might ask whether the present (undoubtedly late) recension of 15:1–6 conceals an earlier narrative whose basic elements were Abraham's lament (in narrative form) and God's promise of a son.

It should be noted that the combination of the two promises appears only in the Abraham narratives, from which we may probably conclude that the promise of the birth of a son belongs particularly to the cycle of Abraham narratives.

The Promise of Many Descendants
Coupled with a Blessing

In one group of passages we find a combination of the promise of many descendants with a blessing (17:16; 17:20; 22:17; 26:4; 26:24; 28:3–4; 32:12; 35:9–12; 48:3–4; 48:16). This large group of passages shows that the promise of many descendants is particularly associated with a blessing. With all their differences, these nine passages have three things in common: (1) the association of blessing and increase; (2) the sequence blessing–increase (that is, the increase is an explication of the blessing); and (3) God as the agent of the blessing and increase.

One of the passages, 48:15–16, records the actual giving of a blessing:

> And he blessed Joseph, and said,
> "The God who . . .
> bless the lads;
> and in them let my name be perpetuated . . . ,
> and let them grow into a multitude in the midst of the earth."

This is a blessing of the type that is appropriate to the death of a father or his departure; there are many examples. The $w^e y i g d \hat{u}$, "let them abound," is meant as an explication of the $y^e b \bar{a} r \bar{e} k$: the blessing results in increase, for blessing is originally the power of fertility. The verb appears only in this passage. The best explanation is that it is a very ancient verb no longer used in the period of the Yahwist and Elohist, and preserved only in this fixed formula.

Genesis 48:15–16 is accordingly a blessing rather than a promise. The increase is intended as the effective result of the power of the blessing. Then we can say with assurance that the origin of the double promise of blessing and increase lies in the act of blessing. Some of the other passages still permit us to see this origin directly.

26:24 I will bless you and multiply your descendants. . . .

22:17 I will indeed bless you,
and I will multiply your descendants as. . . .

In the latest literary stratum, P, the promise of blessing is recast once more in the form of a blessing:

28:3–4 God Almighty bless you
and make you fruitful and multiply you,
that you may become a company of peoples. . . .

See also 35:9–12 and 48:3–4. In this case, however, we cannot escape the conclusion that the promise of increase or many descendants derives from the blessing, that is, from the act of blessing, and is thus by origin not a promise.

But the transformation of the blessing into a promise or the inclusion of the blessing in a promise marked a fundamental change in the concept of blessing. As originally understood, a blessing could not possibly "promise," that is, be announced or predicted for a date in the future. According to the ancient understanding, a blessing takes effect the moment it is pronounced (as in the ancient narratives in chapters 27—28); it cannot promise now and be fulfilled later.[14] By introducing a blessing into the promise in Genesis 12:1–3, the Yahwist transformed an essentially nonhistorical concept into an historical concept; only this change made it possible to do such a thing as promise a blessing and thus also promise increase. In the stories of the patriarchs we can distinguish an earlier use of blessing, in which the blessing takes effect the moment it is pronounced, from a later use, in which blessing and increase are established as prospects for a future time.

It follows, therefore, that we cannot expect to find the promise of many descendants in the earliest narrative strata, since these strata know such increase only as an effect of the blessing, not as a promise.

14. C. Westermann, "The Way of the Promise Through the Old Testament," in B. W. Anderson, ed., *The Old Testament and Christian Faith* (New York: Harper, 1963), pp. 210f.

Several points remain. The passages should be classified further and their mutual relationships more closely defined. The relationship between the two versions of the promise should be studied:

> I will multiply your descendants. . . .
> I will make you a great nation. . . .

It should be shown how further blessing elements became linked with the promise of many descendants, such as the statements "Your descendants shall possess the gate of their enemies" and "By your descendants shall all the nations of the earth bless themselves." These later expansions show that the promise of many descendants was understood through the entire history of its transmission as deriving from a blessing.

The Promise of the Land Alone

The next group of passages comprises Genesis 12:7; 13:14–17; 15:7–21; 24:7; 28:13–15; 50:24. At the end of the Joseph story, Joseph says to his brothers,

> I am about to die; but God will visit you,
> and bring you up out of this land
> to the land which he swore
> to Abraham, to Isaac, and to Jacob (50:24).

In this sentence the Joseph story reaches its goal: the linking of the exodus narrative with the patriarchal narrative.[15] Here is a direct statement that the promise of the land to the patriarchs has as its actual goal the deliverance of Israel from Egypt and the entrance of Israel into Canaan. The words "God will visit you" are a faint allusion to what is said explicitly in Exodus 3:7. This passage is the clearest statement of the function played by the promise of the land for the authors of the Pentateuch; it also

---

15. Commenting on 50:24, von Rad says, "The promise of land to the patriarchs has long since been lost sight of in the Joseph story, and it was also originally foreign to this narrative. But the incorporation of this narrative into the composition of the patriarchal stories meant that it, too, . . . was oriented toward this ultimate goal of all patriarchal stories" (G. von Rad, Genesis [Philadelphia: Westminster, 1961], p. 428).

21

shows clearly that only the promise of the land could have this function, for only the promise of the land can be meant by pāqad, "God will visit you . . . ." In the entrance into Canaan, it is only the ancient promise of the land that finds fulfillment.

This is in line with the observation that at the beginning of Exodus the two promises clearly diverge. Chapter 1 is dominated by the motif of increase, but it is not used as a promise. We read instead that the Israelites increased greatly in Egypt despite all the countermeasures of the Egyptians (1:7, 8, 12, 20). This is a separate and independent narrative motif. Neither do we find any suggestion that the increase of the people in Egypt represents the fulfillment of earlier promises. The promise of the land then reappears quite independently in Exodus 3; here again, however, the context differs from the context of the promise of the land in the patriarchal narratives (see the discussion of Gen. 50:24 above).

This agrees likewise with the observation that in Deuteronomy the promise to the patriarchs is solely the promise of the land, as von Rad points out (*Theologie des Alten Testaments*, vol. 1, p. 172 [not included in the English translation]): "Deuteronomy, which appeals with great frequency to the promise to the patriarchs, understood it only as a promise of the land."

In Genesis 24:7, too, in Abraham's words to his servant, recalling the promise received earlier from God, we find only the promise of the land.

> Yahweh, the God of heaven,
> who took me from my father's house
> and from the land of my birth,
> and who spoke to me
> and swore to me, "To your descendants I will give this land."

In contrast to 50:24, the promise of the land remains here within the family of the patriarchs. This makes it clear that the form of this promise as it appears in 50:24 is preceded by a stage in which the land is promised to the patriarch Abraham. This promise is to be fulfilled by the settling of the sons of Abraham in this land.

It is also clear that this formulation is very similar to 12:1–3. Genesis 24:7 therefore belongs to the late stage of composition, when the patriarchal narratives were being combined into a single whole. In both passages the promise of the land is based on an oath.

In 12:7, the promise has the same wording as in 24:7:

> Then Yahweh appeared to Abram,
> and said, "To your descendants I will give this land."
> So he built there an altar
> to Yahweh, who had appeared to him.

This passage sounds like an allusion to an ancient narrative whose basic elements have been summarized in these sentences, but without the situation that occasioned the promise (see above). A very ancient narrative may be behind this allusion. But when the three actions spoken of here are compared with the genre of the promise of the birth of a son found in Genesis 16 and 18, an essential element is missing in 12:7: the situation that occasions the theophany and promise. If there is really an ancient narrative behind 12:7, we must assume the existence of such a missing element, which is necessary to introduce tension into the train of events. Without such tension it would not be a real narrative. It is quite possible that this missing element might be found in the direction of the intimation in Deuteronomy 26:5: "A wandering [or: 'perishing'] Aramean was my father . . . ." A promise presupposes some exigency or need, such as is suggested here. In our examination of the other passages we must pay particular attention to this element.

Genesis 15:7–21. It has been said of verse 7 that the formulation ". . . who brought you out . . . , to give you this land to possess" probably presupposes the exodus tradition of the nation.[16] In any case, the statement is not a direct promise but an expanded self-introduction: "I am Yahweh, who . . . ." Verse 7 is therefore certainly not the introduction of an ancient promise

---

16. O. Kaiser, "Untersuchung von Gen. 15," and others.

narrative. Next follows a lament, exactly as in 15:1–6. Here, however, the lament itself contains a request for a sign; promise and sign are more closely related than in 15:1–6. There is no need to discuss the ceremony that follows. The event described in verse 17

> Behold, a smoking fire pot and a flaming torch
> passed between these pieces

represents the sign requested by Abraham, by which he knows that he will really receive the land. This event was understood as an oath ceremony. The content of the oath is once again identical in all respects to the simple promise of the land in 12:7 and 24:7, except that here the extent of the territory is added in what is clearly poetry (four doubles).

> To your descendants I give this land,
> from the river of Egypt to the great river.

Now what was said of 12:7 applies also to 15:7ff.: there is no mention of the situation that evokes the events described. Both God's oath and Abraham's lament point to a concrete exigency (cf. God's oath in the judgment discourses of the prophets!). Here, too, the situation may be conjectured along the lines of Deuteronomy 26:5. It is quite possible that this initial situation had to be omitted because the patriarchal narratives depict Abraham already journeying within the land of Canaan; the situation in which Canaan can be the object of desire is no longer really present. We can then assume that Genesis 15:7–21 is based on an ancient narrative telling about the promise of the land, but now greatly revised and modified.

Only in these passages we have just discussed does the promise of the land occur alone in the present text. There are, however, two further passages in which the secondary addition of another promise can be discerned.

In Genesis 13:14–17, verse 16, the promise of many descendants, is certainly a secondary addition, as the structure of the section shows.

14. (Introduction) Yahweh said to Abraham
    (Linkage) after Lot had separated from him,
    (First imperative) "Lift up your eyes from . . . to . . .
15. (Motivation) for all the land . . . I will give to you. . . .
17. (Second imperative) Arise, walk through . . . the land,
    (Motivation) for I will give it to you."

The whole passage is an extended land promise. It is not a narrative, but an address by God to Abraham. The promise is expanded by means of two imperatives which present the promise very nicely in graphic terms: both the command to look (the same stylistic device as in 15:5) and the command to walk presuppose fulfillment. With his eyes and with his feet Abraham is now to take possession of the land that will one day belong to him or his descendants.[17]

The addition of this promise passage to the narrative of Lot's separation from Abraham is secondary but highly appropriate. The separation bears witness to an exigency that appears frequently in the patriarchal narrative: the land can no longer accommodate the growing group, and so division is necessary, as here. This exigency is met by the promise of the land, promising space in abundance, plenty of dwelling space for the coming generations. The section 13:14–17 illustrates especially well the significance the motif of the promise of the land had for the development of the patriarchal stories.[18]

As most scholars assume, 28:13–15 is an interpolation into the theophany at Bethel; verse 16 could follow verse 12 directly, or

17. T. H. Gaster, *Thespis*, 2d ed. (Garden City: Doubleday, 1961), page 193 cites section 40 of the Baal epic, "The Tour of the Dominions"

  (While the) god(s are mak)ing merry on the Mountain,
  while the gods are (regaling themselves) in the North,
  Baal travels from city to city, turns from town to town,
  assumes possession of sixty-six cities . . .

and comments: "This episode mythologizes the very common practice of acquiring territory by ceremonially walking round it. . . ."

18. On 13:14–17, see J. Skinner, *A Critical and Exegetical Commentary on Genesis* (International Critical Commentary, vol. 1, 2d ed. [Edinburgh: Clark, 1930]), page 253: "This solemn assurance of the possession of the land (14—17) is somewhat of a contrast to the simple promise of 12².⁷; and has affinities with a series of passages which appear to represent a later phase of religious reflexion."

the promise section (vv. 13–15) could have replaced something else. In any case, the Bethel narrative was recounted at one time without any promise element.

Verses 13–15 simply join three promises in series: the promise of the land in verse 13, the promise of many descendants in 14a and b, a blessing for all the families of the earth in 14c, and the promise "I will be with you" in 15. That such juxtaposition of quite disparate promises belongs to a later literary stratum is immediately obvious when one realizes that each of them was the outgrowth of a particular situation.[19]

Within verses 13–15, 13 is a self-contained unit which can be taken alone:

> And behold, Yahweh stood above him and said,
> "I am Yahweh, the God of Abraham your father and the God of Isaac;
> the land on which you lie I will give to you and to your descendants."

It is possible that this verse once constituted the nucleus of an independent promise narrative, thus making it a parallel to 12:7. Such a theory is supported by the new introduction, which clashes somewhat with verse 12, and in any case could be the introduction to an independent narrative. It is also supported by

---

19. This assumption applies also to the promise "I will be with you." It certainly has a long prehistory, a very early stage of which can be seen in the Sumerian precursors of the Gilgamesh Epic. In the saga that Kramer calls "Gilgamesh and the Land of the Living," Gilgamesh plans an expedition into the "Land of the Living" and tells Enkidu of his plan. Enkidu advises him to inform the sun god Utu of his plan, because he is the lord of that land. Gilgamesh does so:

He says to Utu of heaven:
"O Utu, I would enter the 'land,' be my ally,
I would enter the land of the cut-down cedar, be my ally."

(S. N. Kramer, History Begins at Sumer [London: Thames & Hudson, 1958], pp. 230ff.). The god's reply is not recorded explicitly—only that it is affirmative. The god Utu promises Gilgamesh that in that land he will be his ally, that he will be by his side. This reply corresponds to the promise "I will be with you." The parallelism between the two situations appears especially in the fact that both cases deal with a journey into a foreign land. It is therefore likely that the Sumerian epic exhibits an early stage of the promise to "be with" someone, such as we find in the patriarchal narratives.

the peculiar formulation of the promise: "the land on which you lie." This fragment might suggest the situation that occasioned the promise: Jacob is a fugitive, spending the night in the open.

So far we have not considered the P passages that contain promises. Although they contain many elements of considerable antiquity (to which occasional reference has been made), they cannot alter the conclusions drawn from the earlier literary strata.[20] One feature, however, is exhibited by all the promise passages in P: the combination or juxtaposition of several promises can be considered with absolute certainty to be a late stage of development. This stage, however, already appears in J in such passages as 28:13-15 and in E in the secondary addition in chapter 22. When we find these late combinations containing several promises, we must continue our inquiry back to the individual promise elements and their particular traditions.

CONCLUSION

The question was: in the narratives of Genesis, can we recognize a specific type or genre of promise narrative? Before this question could be answered, we had to examine another: what was the content of the promise originally—the land, many descendants, or both? It turned out, however, that this did not exhaust the list of possibilities. A survey of all the promises reveals the following possibilities:

The land alone
Descendants alone
The birth of a son alone
Descendants and a son
Descendants and a blessing
Descendants and the land
Several different promises

Examination of these groups within the context of the question stated above yields—in outline—the following results:

20. Pace Hoftijzer, Verheissungen.

1) We can definitely conclude that only one element is promised in the earliest stratum.

2) We found an original promise narrative in which the concern is the promise of (the birth of) a son (Genesis 18 and 16).

3) Very probably there was an original promise narrative that dealt with the promise of the land. It has not been preserved in its original form, but Genesis 15:7–21 may be close to it, as may also an earlier form of Genesis 28.

4) The promise of many descendants was derived originally from a blessing. It is a secondary formation, analogous to the promises of a son and of the land. There are thus no original promise narratives that deal with the increase of descendants.

5) In the course of an extremely rich and varied tradition, these three basic elements—the promise of a son, the promise of the land, blessing and increase—determined the growth and development of the patriarchal history.

6) Finally, there comes the additive combination of several promises, especially in P and in secondary expansions of the ancient narratives.

It turns out, therefore, that only a very small portion of the narratives in Genesis 12—50 were conceived originally as promise narratives. Most of the narratives in which we find promises were transformed secondarily into promise narratives, or else the promises stand outside the ancient narratives as expansions, interpolations, additions, interludes, or special scenes representing the giving of a promise. The promise motif belongs in the vast majority of cases to the stage when the early narratives were being put together to form larger units. To this stage there already belongs the promise framed from the perspective of the growth of the Pentateuch, that is, the promise linking the patriarchal history with the history of the nation, as is formulated most clearly in 50:24.

But this promise linking the history of the patriarchs with that of the nation (as presented by Noth in his A History of Pentateuchal Traditions, see above) was able to draw on an earlier promise motif that the traditionists found already present in the ancient patriarchal narratives themselves. Here not only the promise but also its fulfillment falls in the patriarchal period. It is contained in the promise of the birth of a son and (possibly) in the promise of the land. But the narratives in which this motif was shaped belong to a different category, that of family narrative. These narratives are concerned with the preservation and territory of the family, and will be examined in more detail in what follows.

In addition, we have determined criteria for distinguishing various types or forms of narrative:

(1) A narrative gives literary form to a series of events in which tension is resolved. However the tensions and their resolutions may differ, the shaping of a sequence of events in a narrative somehow always involves the creation of tension and its resolution. Apart from possible exceptions, this can be considered a fundamental criterion: to find the totality of a narrative, one must look first for this arch that binds a sequence of events together, resolving some tension.

(2) A different type was found in Genesis 15:1–6 and 15:7–21. Here, too, a tension and its resolution can be found; but the narrative (and one can still speak here of narrative in a broader sense) did not arise directly out of the literary treatment of a situation imbued with tension, which is then guided toward its resolution. Tension and resolution are instead introduced into a preexisting structure, that of the salvation oracle responding to a lament. The exigency is not part of the narrative; it is expressed in a formal lament.

(3) A totally different type is represented by Genesis 13:14–17. Here we cannot speak of a narrative; the passage has in fact been appended to a finished narrative. It is a kind of scene such as is found only appended to or interpolated within another series of events. Sometimes it is still clearly marked as a scene, as by the introduction in Genesis 22:15: "And the angel of Yahweh called to Abraham a second time from heaven, and said

. . . ." Such an extra scene can have various kinds of structure. Genesis 13:14–17 is a model for how a motif—the motif of the promise of the land—can be expanded into a scene.

(4) A fourth type can be found in Genesis 12:7. This verse is not an interpolation or addition, but a self-contained independent passage, a "minimal unit." Unlike 13:14–17, it cannot be called a motif expanded into a scene. We termed it above an "allusion to a narrative." It is the residuum of what was once a narrative, now vanished. These residua of former narratives in Genesis deserve special attention; in each case we must ask whether it is still possible to determine the genre of the "vanished narrative" and the reasons why it vanished. In this case (Gen. 12:7) I think we can determine the reason. The situation that gave rise to the narratives of the promise of the land no longer obtains in the patriarchal stories; the patriarchs are already dwelling in Canaan, albeit without fixed abode.

This survey is not meant to describe all the narrative types appearing in this area. But the four we have described can be recognized with certainty and can serve for further orientation.

II
Basic Questions on the Genesis Narratives

STARTING POINT: NOTH'S A HISTORY OF PENTATEUCHAL TRADITIONS

When we review the presentation of the patriarchal history in Martin Noth's A History of Pentateuchal Traditions, we find that the interest of this traditio-historical presentation focuses first on the theme of the promise to the patriarchs, which determines the entire patriarchal history; then on the cultic sites as the loci of sagas or saga cycles; and finally on the "human figures in the narrative" (§9). The individual narratives and what takes place in them receive notably less attention.

There is also a second aspect. Within these three areas of interest, Noth focuses repeatedly on what is concretely historical: places and regions, persons and the groups represented by these persons, traditio-historical relationships with possible bearing on historical relationships. In the presentation as a whole, the postulate that we are not dealing with history in the stories of the patriarchs appears in surprising conjunction with a traditio-historical inquiry for which historical criteria are crucial: names, places, historical relationships. By contrast, Noth pays almost no attention to the form of society within which the events of these stories take place and the functions of this form of society. These questions have to be regarded as unimportant in view of Noth's historically oriented interest, because the form of society in which these narratives are set is avowedly prehistorical: the form of family and clan. What takes place within them has, historically speaking, usually no significance.

In my opinion, however, we cannot ignore this form of society and its functions if we wish to understand the patriarchal stories. We must first take the step of setting them radically free from our categories of historical understanding and let them speak in their own world, which is prehistorical.

THREE ICELANDIC NARRATIVE TYPES (JOLLES)

The first part of our study has shown that, of the many passages containing a promise to the fathers, only a very few belong to what were originally promise narratives. In other words, the overwhelming majority of the narratives in the patriarchal stories cannot be understood as originating with the theme of "the promise to the patriarchs"; this theme is associated with the later stages of the tradition. In many narratives, such as the separation from Lot, the sacrifice of Isaac, and the dream at Bethel, the words of promise were not added until the narrative was already in existence as a self-contained unit. These narratives therefore came into being for the most part without any contact with the theme "promise to the patriarchs." The early stages, the stages during which the patriarchal stories were coming into being, are concerned with the life of the family or clan.

It must be stated here at the outset that we will misunderstand this theme, the background of the patriarchal stories, if we view family and clan from our perspective as one domain of human society. We must rather attempt to understand it as the totality of human social life. For these narratives, the larger and more inclusive realms of nation, state, religious community, and cultural field did not yet exist. These realms were beyond the horizon within which the patriarchs lived. But this fact transforms everything. The birth of a child means something else in a modern metropolis than it does in a small village; it is something else in the way of life we are familiar with than in the situation where there is as yet no continuity of human existence apart from the family. Another example: In a way of life for which war (that is, war between nations) does not yet exist, a quarrel (like that between Jacob and Laban) means something else than a quarrel in our world. At that time a quarrel truly played the role of war.

The patriarchal stories concerning the life of the family and clan therefore do not deal with a private or circumscribed domain; they deal rather with the way of life in family and clan that constituted the total existence of those who lived then. The patriarchal stories tell of a prehistorical way of life, and are to be understood in this sense.

In my opinion, Jolles[21] has provided the fundamental description of this narrative form. He finds in the Icelandic sagas the two primary groups we are dealing with in the narratives of Genesis.

---

21. André Jolles, *Einfache Formen* (Halle: Niemeyer, 1930; 5th ed., 1974).

(In the Old Norse saga genre) we are dealing with three groups. The first comprises narratives about the Icelandic settlers, their neighbors and contemporaries, their lineage, their relationships, and the natural and supernatural phenomena they encounter. Far from recounting the history of how the Norwegians took possession of Iceland, these stories all deal with individuals, who, as individuals, belong in turn to families. We hear how a family built a house and farm, how the family wealth increased, how the family came into contact with other families in the same district, how they quarreled, became reconciled, feuded or lived in peace, how many sons and daughters the family had, where the sons got their wives, into which families the daughters married. Sometimes the family is represented as a person, its head; sometimes it appears as a whole. These narratives are fast-moving; there is nothing but action. . . .

A second group does not deal with family history in the narrow sense, but with royal narratives. These royal narratives, however, are far removed from what we call political history. . . .

In addition to these groups, there is a third, which goes far beyond what we found in the first and second. In the first place, it is far less restricted in space and time; it includes and uses materials going back long before the settlement of Iceland. . . . And finally these narratives go ever further and recount things that, generally speaking, we associate with our genres that begin: "Long ago and far away." But . . . they present these materials in such a way that they cannot be separated from the previous materials; they narrate them in a sense as though the persons were the same and the events comparable with what befell a family of settlers in Iceland. . . . These we call "sagas of long ago" (pp. 67–68).

In the first and third groups we have, in my opinion, precise counterparts to the patriarchal history and primal history in Genesis. The mutual relationship between both is the same. In the description of the first group, every single statement applies to the patriarchal stories in Genesis and can be attested in the narratives of Genesis 12–50. Above all, however, we find here an explanation of why the narratives of the primal history in Genesis—although we are dealing with a totally different realm— are so similar to those of the patriarchal history. This relationship is now defined more precisely:

Contrary to what is generally accepted, Andreas Heusler (*Die Anfänge der isländischen Saga*, Berlin, 1914) demonstrated convincingly that form a had to constitute the point of departure for the others. The actual saga form as it developed in Iceland during a specific period is the form we find in the family stories of the first group. There it took shape. Later it came to include other materials, but it always preserved its original form. Heusler shows further that this form came into being orally and became so established in its oral form that it could be transferred to written form without difficulty (p. 69).

Applied to Genesis, this would mean that the patriarchal narratives came first, and that the narratives of the so-called primal history were framed after the patriarchal stories. This would explain their similarities.[22]

In the detailed description of the first group, a crucial point is made that applies also to the patriarchal narratives. "These sagas show how history exists only as family history." "The inner structure of the *Islendinga Saga* is determined by the concept of the family." Concepts determinative of family life such as "blood relationship, marriage, kindred, inheritance, and heritability here form the framework." Thus the events narrated in Genesis (or the narratives in which they are recounted) take on, as it were, another dimension. They are no longer what we call "private life" or events in the private sphere; this sphere here becomes *public*. Politics, economics, culture, and religion here become family matters and cease to exist except in family events. There is nothing significant that takes place outside this sphere.

The extent to which family concepts and events constitute the framework of the patriarchal stories can be observed initially in the fact that in the three sections of the patriarchal history various family relationships clearly stand in the foreground. In the

---

22. I would also raise the question whether the second type of saga, here called royal narrative, is not represented in the Old Testament, namely in the stories of the Judges. This would explain why the stories of Judges exhibit so many similarities in narrative style to the patriarchal stories. But only comparison in detail could demonstrate this.

Abraham cycle (12—25) the events involve the relationship between parent and child; in the Jacob—Esau cycle (25—36), they involve the relationship between two brothers; in the Joseph cycle, we have a complex series of events involving a father, a brother, and a circle of brothers. These complex events are reflected in the complex form of the novella; in the first two cycles, simple narrative predominates.

The significance of the fact that the prehistorical tradition of Israel consists essentially of family narrative can be seen even more clearly when one takes into account the fact that the hero saga never developed in Israel—or, if it did exist at one time, it was not preserved and left only traces in the traditions still extant. The narratives of Judges stand in a certain proximity to the hero saga, but they are something fundamentally different. The absence of true hero sagas is particularly apparent in comparison to the literature of Mesopotamia. The Gilgamesh Epic is an outgrowth of the hero saga, and in what remains of Sumerian literature the hero saga plays a very important part. Herein lies one of the most important differences between the early traditions of the Old Testament and Babylonian/Sumerian literature.[23]

---

23. For this reason I prefer the term "narratives" to the term "sagas" in Genesis. Unlike the Icelandic word saga, the German word Sage is traditionally associated so closely with the hero saga that to a German audience the word Sage immediately suggests hero saga. But this would place the narratives of Genesis in a false light from the outset. I am in complete agreement with Gunkel's basic thesis that "Genesis is a collection of sagas"; nor do I have any objection to taking "saga" as a general term embracing family saga and hero saga. It must be clear from the outset, however, that the narratives of Genesis are not hero sagas, but represent a fundamentally different genre. The difference is especially clear in one point: the family narrative knows nothing of the most important motif in the hero saga, in which the hero strives to perform great deeds and thus strives after honor. In the Gilgamesh Epic, the hero wishes to make a name for himself through his deeds:

> The "lord" Gilgamesh, realizing that, like all mortals, he must die sooner or later, is determined at least to "raise up a name" for himself before he meets his destined end. He therefore sets his heart on journeying to the far-distant "Land of the Living," with the probable intention . . . (S. N. Kramer, History Begins at Sumer [London: Thames & Hudson, 1958], pp. 174–75).

Then read what Kramer describes in the same book in the chapter "Man's First Heroic Age," and consider the opening verses of the Niebelungenlied: this is a world totally different from that of the patriarchal stories!

THE ETIOLOGIES

What is the relationship between the etiologies and the family narratives? What is an etiology or an etiological narrative? If an etiology answers a question about the origin of something or someone, this still does not have anything to say about the nature or genre of the narrative that answers the question. In other words, the category of etiology must initially be kept distinct from the question of the types of narrative in Genesis. The narrative answer to a question about the origin of something or someone can vary extensively; or else this question of origins can be dealt with in a sentence or two, which cannot be termed a narrative but only a note or the like.

Let us take as our starting point the basic form of narrative described in our discussion of the promise narratives: a narrative gives literary form to a sequence of events leading from tension to its resolution. Then an etiological narrative of this type can only be one in which the path from the question prompting the etiology to the answer that gives the etiological conclusion coincides with the arch that runs from tension to resolution. But there is also a wealth of other possibilities, in which the line of narrative answer to a question does not coincide with the narrative line, down to an answer in a mere note or etiological comment, which is far removed from a true narrative.

In order to pursue the question further, we must begin with Gunkel, because, as far as I can see, there has been since Gunkel's introduction to his commentary on Genesis (first published in 1901; now *Genesis*, 7th ed. [Göttingen: Vandenhoeck and Ruprecht, 1966]) no equally comprehensive and systematic presentation of the etiologies.

In §1, Gunkel explains his basic thesis: "Genesis is a collection of sagas." In §2, he discusses the types of saga in Genesis, taking as his starting point the basic distinction between (a) the sagas of the primal age and (b) the sagas of the patriarchs. This distinction agrees in every detail with the two primary groups of

sagas that Jolles finds in the Icelandic sagas (see above). Apart
from a few suggestive comments, there does not follow, as one
would expect, a further classification of the types of saga in
Genesis. Some general observations are made about the primal
sagas and the patriarchal sagas; then comes point 7, "The Etiological Motifs." Within this section we find a classification—
not, however, a classification of the types of saga, but one of the
various etiological motifs: (a) ethnological; (b) etymological;
(c) cultic; and (d) geological. In sections 8 and 9, Gunkel
stresses once more that only rarely and exceptionally can the
types of the sagas be determined by such motifs. On the one
hand, "various motifs are almost always combined in the sagas,"
and "the etymological motifs in particular never appear independently in the earlier sagas"; on the other, Gunkel would
prefer to find the nucleus of the narratives (frequently or always?) not in the interpretable etiological motifs, but rather
"that which we cannot interpret is in each case the nucleus of
the narrative" (section 9).

From this presentation one would conclude that it is impossible to determine the types of the Genesis sagas solely on the
basis of etiological motifs. Of course it is possible, like Gunkel, to
speak of a cultic saga when a motif of cultic etiology is clearly
present. But this is certainly not possible in each instance, and
a cultic saga never is indicated solely by the motif of a cultic
etiology!

More caution is advisable in terming a narrative an etiology.
Etiological narratives play a very important role in the narratives
of Genesis, in their development and in their final form. But it
is not appropriate to call a narrative containing one or more
etiological motifs an etiology or an etiological saga simply on
account of this fact. This is possible only when the line of the
narrative coincides totally with the line of the etiology. To repeat
as emphatically as possible: there is no such thing as a pure etiology or an etiological saga. In other words, the answer to a
question about the origin or basis of a present circumstance is

not, as such, a saga. This answer can consist merely of a very brief statement or explanation; even a detailed explanation of the circumstance in question is not, as such, a saga. An essentially different element must be added to turn such an answer into a saga, the element that constitutes a narrative in the strict sense. Gunkel gives in passing the same definition of the essential nature of a narrative as is given here. Speaking of actions (section 16), he says at one point, "When there is no tension at all, when there are no complications, we do not have a story in the true sense" (p. xlvii). But this tension, which must be present if there is to be a real story (the distinction between "complications" and "tension" remains to be defined), is not contained in the etiological motif as such; it must be added and associated with the motif.

This point, however, is not clearly made by Gunkel. Shortly after the passage just quoted, he takes up the etiological motif once more and says (section 17, p. xlix):

> Many of the sagas answer specific questions; their purpose is to instruct. . . . In the Hagar narrative, all the weight falls on the resolving sentence: God heard (21:17). This impression is deliberate on the part of the narrator; it was his purpose to build on this word his explanation of the name Ishmael. Or in Genesis 22:8 "God provided."

The two narratives cited here as examples certainly do not have instruction as their primary purpose! Neither does this statement agree at all with Gunkel's subsequent explanation in his exegesis. He already betrays himself when he speaks of the "resolving sentence" in the Hagar narrative. What is resolved is the tension arising from the narrative of the peril to mother and child, not the question of how the name Ishmael is to be explained. The same is true in Genesis 22; there is no need to go into detail. Gunkel's unclear explanation was possible only because in these very narratives the line of the question and its answer coincides so strikingly with the line of the narrative proper in which tension is resolved; therein lies a particular refinement, therein is revealed a particularly high narrative art. But these very examples make it abundantly clear that it is something other than the etiology that provides the tension and resolution in the story.

In defining the types of narrative in Genesis, then, we will initially disregard any group of "etiological sagas" (or narratives) and, like Gunkel himself, include etiology among the motifs. Then, when we encounter an etiological motif, the first and most important question will be what function it has in each particular case in the textual unit where it appears, and what this unit represents apart from the etiological motif. This question is more important for determining the nature of the textual unit than is the question of what is the group to which the etiological motif belongs. A grouping of the narratives according to the etiological motifs they contain, dividing them into etymological or ethnographic or geological sagas, is actually impossible, and not productive in any case.

As a consequence, caution is advisable with regard to any sweeping judgment about the nature of etiologies. We must no longer view etiologies so superficially as to conclude that the question about a place, a practice, a natural phenomenon, or a cultural relic gave rise to the answer given in the narrative, in other words, that this answer was made up. The etiologies must instead be viewed in perspective. The narrative answering the question or the etiological line within this narrative represents in each case a bridge from the known to the unknown. This can be done in many different ways, and therefore the relationship of question to answer, of known to unknown, can differ widely. In each case we must search afresh for the path from the question to the answer. The question must be evaluated variously depending on the nature of the context in which the etiological motif occurs. An etiological question in the realm of the family narrative is something fundamentally different from an etiological question in the realm of the primal history, which deals with questions of human existence. An etiological question in historical narrative is again something totally different. The realm in which the question is raised is much more important for our evaluation of an etiological motif than is the classification of its subject matter, which in any case, as Gunkel's survey clearly shows, causes serious difficulties.

The etiological motif would never have come into being and could never have acquired such importance in the composition of sagas if it had not been preceded by a form in which the path from the question to the answer could be seen at a glance, so that the answer had the same degree of reality as the question. In the Old Testament, this is obviously the case in those passages where only one generation lies between question and answer. When children ask a question about the reasons for a phenomenon they encounter, the answer the parents give is trustworthy. It must be trustworthy. Etiologies begin with trustworthy answers, not made up ones. The discussion of etiology in a series of recent studies exhibits for the most part an avoidance of general and abstract definitions and a striving for differentiation and precision.

A brief survey of the discussion between John Bright and Martin Noth on the historical significance of etiological narratives is in order. Their debate suffers from the fact that both of them start with imprecise definitions of etiology and the etiological factor. Its value lies primarily in the fact that they both move in the direction of a more precise and nuanced definition of "etiology."

In his *Early Israel in Recent Historical Writing* (Studies in Biblical Theology 19 [Chicago: Allenson, 1956]), pages 91ff., Bright argues against the emphasis placed by the Alt-Noth school "upon aetiology as a creative factor in the formation of tradition." He offers instead the thesis "that, where historical tradition is concerned, not only can it be proved that the aetiological factor is often secondary in the formation of these traditions, it cannot be proved that it was ever primary."

As an example of the evaluation of etiology that he rejects, he cites above all Alt's treatment of Joshua 1—9 ("Josua," in his

Kleine Schriften, vol. 1 [Munich: Beck, 1953], pp. 176–192).
He concludes,

> The gravity of all this lies in the fact that, in the minds of Alt
> and Noth, when the aetiological factor is present in a tradition,
> that tradition is automatically suspect. It could hardly be his-
> torical, for the aetiological factor created it . . . (Bright, *Early
> Israel*, p. 92).

The crucial question is not whether the etiological factor is
present in such narratives, but "the priority of that factor in the
formation of tradition." To answer this question, Bright differ-
entiates the appearance of the etiological factor in various literary
forms. For fable and fairy tale he recognizes that the etiological
factor can often be the creative and determinative element. For
myth, the case is less clear. And it is no longer true at all for "the
traditions of the great Hebrew historical saga," the national traditions of Israel (p. 92). This statement can be made if it can be
demonstrated in other national traditions that narratives with
etiological motifs are historical in spite of these etiological features. Bright illustrates the point by means of a series of narratives from the early history of America (pp. 93–100).

We may concur with Bright in his statement that the etiological factor as such cannot determine whether the events of the
narrative actually took place or not. We may also agree that the
etiological factor must not be isolated; in each case we must ask
in what genre the etiological motif is found and what function it
has in the narrative under discussion. An etiological motif can
thus be evaluated differently in different contexts with reference
to the question of historicity. The position taken by Noth in his
response (see below) does not differ essentially on these two
points. It means a significant advance when unanimity is achieved
on these points. This would mean, of course, that the generalized
hypothesis as formulated by Alt in his article on Joshua (see
above) cannot be maintained as stated. Alt had formulated it as
follows ("Josua," pp. 184–85):

We must return to our conclusion (already worked out by Gressmann in his commentary on Joshua) that the sagas of Joshua 1—11 were originally etiological in character, and ask what this implies for their historical utilization. Obviously something most decisive! If the essence of an etiological saga consists in its purpose of deriving a present circumstance causally from an event of the past, the present circumstance is indubitably an item of historical reality. Nothing is said, however, nor can anything be said, on the basis of the saga in question, as to whether the past event as told in explanation is likewise derived from the realm of historical reality. This applies to the etiological sagas of the Book of Joshua no less than to those of Genesis and all others. . . .

In response, Noth clearly refused to go along with such a generalized evaluation of the "etiological saga" ("Der Beitrag der Archäologie zur Geschichte Israels," *Supplements to Vetus Testamentum: Congress Volume,* Oxford, 1959, vol. 7 [Leiden: Brill, 1960], pp. 262–82). He distinguishes (pp. 279f.) between a narrative "whose purpose is to account for a circumstance that is still observable 'to this day,' i.e., down to the time this narrative was formulated," and "narratives that trace a situation or practice back to venerable antiquity, without aiming at a specific etiological explanation" (p. 279, n. 1). He stresses that the formula "to this day" is not conclusive by itself; it all depends on the nature of the narrative. An etiology can also be a motif in a different kind of narrative. In each particular case, it is an open question how much the substance of the narrative has to do with history. Above all, he clearly admits the possibility "that an accurate historical tradition can become an etiological narrative" (citing W. F. Albright, "The Israelite Conquest of Canaan in the Light of Archaeology," *BASOR* 74 [1939]: 12ff.). It is therefore impossible to claim that the position of Noth as just outlined is affected by Bright's criticism on this point. The most important difference is that even in the case of an historical narrative Noth allows for the possibility that the narrative is an outgrowth of etiological invention, whereas Bright would exclude it a priori. Noth concludes this section with a statement that Bright would certainly accept: "We must reckon with a whole range of possibilities."

This indicates the direction we must go in pursuing our inquiry into the significance of the etiological motif in the various realms of narrative and report. How such nuanced inquiry can lead to a history of the etiological motif in these various realms is shown by two additional valuable studies devoted to etiology: J. Fichtner, "Die etymologische Ätiologie in den Namengebungen der geschichtlichen Bücher des Alten Testaments," *Vetus Testamentum* 6 (1956), pages 372–96; and B. S. Childs, "A Study of the Formula 'Until this Day,' " *Journal of Biblical Literature* 82 (1963), pages 279–92. Both mark an advance, in that, examining etiology within its larger context, they present its form and function with many more nuances than heretofore, thus exhibiting stages in the history of the motif.

Fichtner works out two basic forms of naming: the first, a name followed by its motivation (etymological etiology); the second, the formula "and therefore he was called . . ." concluding an event. Even this distinction of two forms, which is fundamental to the study, shows that naming can be related to the narrative in different ways: "Form I in accounts that explicitly lead up to the naming . . . form II, when we are dealing with an account of a significant event, which led in turn to the naming" (p. 381). Fichtner does not go into the relationship of the naming to the various types of narrative, but suggests (p. 381) that this area deserves further study: "The most immediate task is to trace the course followed by each etiology with its related traditions until it appears in its present form."

Childs limits his study to the formula "until this day," and finds that it exhibits quite different uses. It turns out that the formula as such does not mark a narrative as an etiology in every case. For example (p. 285), "In the remaining examples of etymological etiologies with the formula there is not a single clear example in which the etiology provides the main focal point about which the traditions cluster." In all these cases we must rather conclude that ". . . the essential connection between the event and the etiology has been dissolved" (p. 285). Childs comes to the conclusion: "In the great majority of cases, the formula 'until this day' has been secondarily added." Without discussing this result in further detail, we can say that in any case the study has certainly demonstrated that narratives containing etiological motifs must not be called "etiological sagas" simply for that reason. In each case we must inquire into the "focal point about which the traditions cluster."

The same direction is taken by J. L. Seeligmann, "Aetiological Elements in Biblical Historiography" [Hebrew with English summary], *Zion* 26 (1961), pages 141–69, also noted in *IZBG* 9 (1962/63), page 35. Seeligmann, too, comes to the conclusion that the historicity of a tradition is independent of its etiological character, that the etiologies must be evaluated quite variously depending on their context, and that the etiological element is a secondary addition to many narratives.

III

Narratives of Crime and Punishment in Genesis 1—11

There is a type of narrative in Genesis that tells of a crime and its punishment, roughly corresponding to the theme of Dostoevski's novel. It must be stated at the outset, however, that there is no word for "punishment" in Hebrew; the name given these narratives above is conceived from our own perspective.

The only pure and complete example of a crime/punishment narrative in Genesis is Genesis 2—3, but the motif appears throughout the whole primal history: crime and punishment are mentioned in Genesis 4; 6:1–4; 6—8; (9:20–27); 11:1–9. We are therefore justified in speaking of a basic motif fundamental to the primal history. The same motif appears in the patriarchal history, but not in such a way that narratives are structured upon it. At best it is wholly or partly determinative in the story of Joseph, but here the primary emphasis is characteristically not on the sequence of crime and punishment, but of crime and forgiveness. When crime and punishment appear in chapters 12–36, the theme is never expressly that of crime leading necessarily to punishment.[24]

Genesis 2–3 is a perfect model of the crime/punishment narrative because the events leading from the one to the other determine the structure of the narrative. We are told how the crime comes to be committed; then, following the immediate consequences of the crime, comes the prosecution. Between the crime and its punishment stand the discovery of the deed and the examination of the criminals, both presented in detail. The unique feature of this narrative is that God himself both discovers the crime and prosecutes the criminals. Only here in the entire Bible do we find the direct statement that God punishes a human crime, in such a way that the prosecution and punishment are carried out in all their details by God himself, as though God and man shared a common space, as though crime, prosecution, and punishment all took place on the same level.[25] Only in Genesis 4 do we find anything similar, and even here only in abbreviated and allusive form. Nevertheless, in Genesis 4 discovery and trial also come between crime and punishment, both carried out directly by God.[26, 27]

24. For example, in the brief passage Genesis 38:6–10. The situation is quite different in the curse on Simeon and Levi (Gen. 49:5–7); see also the Reuben aphorism in verses 3–4.

25. Nothing like this reappears until the scenes of universal judgment of the apocalyptic tradition (for example, Matthew 25).

26. The parallel structure demonstrates that Genesis 3 and Genesis 4 belong together.

27. It may be objected that what is actually manifest in these narratives of the primal history is man's sin and God's grace. And this is in fact how we hear these stories, but we are hearing them on the basis of our own preconceived ideas. But if we let each of these narratives speak totally for itself, the truly determinative acts come into focus: (a) An individual or group commits a misdeed, usually a transgression of the limits imposed on man. (b) The misdeed has the potential

The punishments fall into two groups. In Genesis 3, the punishments are circumstances that are now present and, within the limits of experience, have always been present: the shape of the serpent, the thorns in the field, the pain of childbirth. These circumstances are explained by the narrative. This group appears also to include Genesis 6:1–4 (span of life). In the other group the punishment is a unique event, a catastrophe: Genesis 6–8 and 19 (also 19:26, Lot's wife), as well as 11. In both groups, however, the punishment remains within the realm of the created world or natural phenomena; as lord of creation, God punishes by a direct action not mediated through historical forces (as in Isaiah, "rod of my anger").

In both groups the origin of these stories must have involved reflection on the how and why of such catastrophes or such limitations on human or natural life, perceived as curses. Neither the "permanent" nor the "sudden" causes of distress are simply accepted. The narratives inquire into their origins and, hence, their meaning. Thus the crime/punishment narratives point to a specific intellectual occupation (Jolles), the investigation of origins; in other words, these are etiological narratives. But this does not really explain how these narratives came into being. In all of them the inquiry pursues a specific course: the fact or situation points in every case to a crime; the path that leads from the crime as the initial circumstance to the fact or situation under investigation is in each case the path of personal prosecution. In each case the crime is punished by the personal God who sees (or discovers) it and pursues the course of justice. The question of origins is associated from the outset—and that means in the very first sketch of these narratives—with the crime/punishment motif, or, more precisely, with talk of God as the one who sees trans-

---

to destroy the limit totally. (c) Then the reaction sets in; in each story it involves a direct action on the part of God, in every case imposing a restraint on man as he attempts to break out. That is the basic structure of the sequence of events. Only afterwards, imposing a limit on this punishment, do we find an act of God's mercy, allowing the criminal to remain alive—under restraint.

gressions and punishes them. God is spoken of in this fashion even in the latest period, as when the prophet Zechariah, being stoned to death, cries out, "May Yahweh see and avenge!"

Furthermore, all these question arise within a particular sphere. In all the narratives which belong here, the narration moves within the broadest realm conceivable, the realm of humankind or of all creation. When such a narrative is localized, its setting is somewhere in the world outside of Israel: the garden of Eden to the east, the cities at the southern end of the Dead Sea, the tower in Babylon, the ark on Mount Ararat. Thus the questions arise within the sphere of the world and humankind.

Just because the setting is so broad, totally different solutions or answers would be possible to the same questions. Suffering or catastrophe might well be caused by other powers, hostile to God! Such narratives or narrative explanations of existing circumstances are found in incalculable number in other religions. But this type of explanation does not exist for Israel. It is quite clear that etiological narratives of this sort were known in Israel; their echoes can often be heard through the biblical narratives, for example, the hostility of the serpent to God in Genesis 3. But the crime/punishment narratives in Genesis stand in sharp contrast to such explanations. Behind them all stands the recognition that there cannot be any ultimately causative powers besides Yahweh. In this sense, these narratives of the primal history are all based on the fundamental theological principle that it is Yahweh alone who brings to pass, that Yahweh alone is God. What was conceptualized much later in Deuteronomy 6:4 is already present behind the conception of these crime/punishment narratives: "Yahweh our God, Yahweh is one." Because all the evil in the world and in human life can come only from Yahweh, the evil that is encountered or acknowledged in these narratives is traced back to God in such a way as to indicate God's punitive intervention, in response to a crime that God saw and avenged. In the crime/punishment narratives this answer, rooted in the belief in

God's uniqueness, took on form. Their special feature is that this answer is ventured for the origin of evil in the broadest sphere of the world and humankind.[28]

The Individual Narratives[29]

THE PLACE OF THE CRIME/PUNISHMENT NARRATIVES IN GENESIS 1—11

A glance reveals the surprising situation that *all* the real narratives in Genesis 1—11 belong to this group.

1:1—2:4a		
	I. 2:4b—3:24	Humanity: creation and transgression
	II. 4:1–16	Cain and Abel
4:17–24		
4:25–26		
5:1–32		
	III. 6:1–4	Origin of the giants
	IV. 6:5—9:17	Deluge
9:18–20	(VI. 9:20–27	Canaan's misdeed and curse)
10:1–32		
	V. 11:1–9	Tower of Babel
11:10–26		
(11:27–32)		

28. H. Gunkel, *Genesis übersetzt und erklärt* ([Göttinger] Handkommentar zum Alten Testament" I/1, 7th ed. [Göttingen: Vandenhoeck & Ruprecht, 1966]), page 1: "Thus this primal history speaks . . . of the sin of man . . . and the wrath of God, who expelled man from the garden . . . uprooted . . . dispersed; at the same time, however, it speaks of the grace and mercy of the Most High, . . . A primal history of humankind of a religious and ethical grandeur, to which other nations have nothing comparable."

29. The following discussion is merely an outline, not claiming to be complete in any respect. Its purpose is to suggest a new perspective for the explanation of the Genesis narratives; it will need further support and confirmation. Discussion of the literature is limited to a minimum.

All the texts in the right column tell of a crime and its punishment, however they may differ in other respects. The other texts —apart from the P creation account, which cannot be called a real narrative—contain only genealogies or expanded genealogies.[30]

The genealogies have been intelligently and artfully combined with the crime/punishment narrative to form a whole. This combination must itself have a lengthy history, because the Sumero-Babylonian myths such as the Enuma Elish exhibit the same association with genealogies, in this case the genealogies of the gods. In Genesis 1–11, the history of the world and humankind is represented as being determined by two fundamental circumstances: (a) Humankind was created with the world and upon the world to live by generations, limited by birth and death. This form of life includes increase and division from generation to generation. (b) From the very outset, human life includes offenses and transgressions. Such offenses and transgressions demand from the very outset and for all humankind a restricting vengeance or punishment on the part of God. This second basic feature is given shape in the crime/punishment narratives.

THE STRUCTURE OF THESE NARRATIVES

The five (or six) narratives share a common basic structure only in the two primary features that are obvious: they all speak of a transgression and its punishment.[31] A third common element,

30. With respect to the Priestly creation account, it is worth noting that its prototype in the Babylonian epic Enuma Elish likewise is a crime/punishment narrative: Tiamat, from whose sundered body heaven and earth were created, was the leader of the rebel gods against whom the divine council under Anu sent the god Marduk.

There is a need to study the crime/punishment motif as a narrative motif in the ancient Near Eastern context of Israel. It is clearly a mythological motif, which Israel excised radically from its mythological context. But this is merely a single aspect, which does not suffice to define the relationship.

It would also be enlightening to compare the prototypes of the Greek tragedies, in which the crime/punishment motif dominates everything.

31. Skinner finds the same structure in chapters 3 and 4: "In both we have the same sequence of sin, investigation and punishment (in the form of a curse)" (Genesis, vol. 1, 2d ed. [Edinburgh: Clark, 1930], p. 100).

albeit not as fixed, is the fact that in each case the punishment consists of an action and a verbal expression of the punishment or the decision to impose it.

	2—3	4:1–16	6:1–4	6—9	11:1–9	(9:20–27)
Transgression	3:6	4:8b	6:1–2	6:5–7	11:4	9:22
Verbal Expression	3:14–19	4:11–12	6:3	6:5–7	11:6–7	9:24–25
Act of Punishment	3:22–24	4:16b		7:6–24	11:8–9	

Besides the points already made, this common structure also expresses the fact that the sequence transgression–punishment includes of necessity a third, verbal element. In none of the narratives does the punishment follow the transgression automatically. The execution of the punishment is instead always preceded by its verbal expression, either directly in words spoken by God to the transgressor (in I and II) or as God's decision (in III—V). This speech or decision in each case relates the punishment to the transgression.

3:14: Because you have done this, cursed are you . . . .

17: Because you have listened . . . cursed is the ground . . . .

4:11: And now you are cursed from the ground, which has opened its mouth to receive your brother's blood . . . .

6:3: Then Yahweh said, "My spirit shall not abide . . . for he is flesh, but his days shall be . . . ."

6:5–7: Yahweh saw that the wickedness of man was great . . . and Yahweh was sorry . . . so Yahweh said, "I will blot out man . . . ."

13: And God said to Noah, "I have determined to make an end of all flesh; for the earth is filled with violence through them;

behold, I will destroy them with the earth" (compare v. 17).

11:6–7: And Yahweh said, "Behold, they are one people ...

and this is only the beginning of what they will do ....

Come, let us go down, and there confuse their language ...."

In each case, these statements constitute the midpoint of the narrative. The words spoken by Yahweh (this introduction is almost identical throughout) each time express a causal relationship; the verbal statement of the punishment is expressly motivated by a transgression. In other words, all these narratives focus on the punishment pronounced by Yahweh in response to a transgression.

We discussed above the first fundamental element of these narratives: the confession of the one God, from whom alone all the evil found in the world of humankind and nature can come. Now we come to the second element: this one God is judge. He imposes limits on the transgressions and misdeeds that form part of human life from the very outset by punishing the transgressions with reason; that is, the punishment is reasonable and therefore judicious. This second theological component likewise stands in sharpest contrast to the rest of the ancient Near East, as is shown especially by the story of the deluge: the "wrath" of God (a word that is never used in the primal history) is never to be explained from the perspective of the divine sphere on the basis of some sequence of events involving the gods and usually reflecting a quarrel, envy, or jealousy. The explanation is almost always exclusively historical, that is, based on events that take place among humans. In his punishment, God acts as judge of humankind. This judicial office necessarily includes a verbal element: a sentence must be pronounced before it can be executed.

SOME OBSERVATIONS ON THE TRANSGRESSIONS
AND THE PUNISHMENT

(a) There are quite a few other similarities and points of agreement, but on the whole the unique features of the individual narratives predominate. The most important difference is that in I and II the transgression is committed by an individual, whereas in III—V it is committed by a group. The effect of this difference on the structure of the narrative is that only I and II can contain a discovery and hearing of the guilty party, for neither is possible in the case of a group. It is of the essence of a judicial hearing that only a single individual is put on trial; if several are charged, each must receive his own sentence, as is the case in Genesis 3. But when a vaguely defined group commits the transgression, as in III, IV, and V, the narrative must take on a different form and Yahweh's judicial office must be depicted differently. Therefore in III, IV, and V the sentence, which is pronounced directly to the guilty party, is replaced by the statement of God's decision to punish or destroy.[32]

(b) The transgression is different in each narrative. In I, it is the violation of a commandment given by God. When the narrator looks upon this as fundamental to the relationship between God and his new creature, he is obviously also saying that this is also the fundamental nature of transgression. The second narrative refers to the most extreme form of a misdeed committed by one person against another. There is no preceding commandment of God, because the narrator wishes to express the fact that the human knows this limit as human.

In III the crime can hardly be defined. The passage is a fragment and also contains several strata. Apparently the sons of the

---

32. The same distinction reappears later in a totally different context: the distinction between the prophetic announcement of judgment to an individual and the announcement to a group (the nation or a group within the nation). Here, too, investigation and hearing (stylized) are possible only in the case of a judgment pronounced to an individual; see C. Westermann, *Basic Forms of Prophetic Speech* (Philadelphia: Westminster, 1967), p. 144.

gods transgress by forming unions with human women. But it is not clear that this act is in fact condemned. In verse 3, the punishment is imposed not on the sons of the gods but on humankind. No clear transgression on the part of humankind is reported, however. It is only suggested that in the children of these unions humankind transgresses its appointed limits. But the whole affair remains vague and obscure.[33] Likewise, in V a transgression of limits appears to be involved, but here, too, its nature is not quite clear. What is clear is that the transgression referred to in chapter 11 was brought about by human labor, by "civilization." In IV, the transgression ("wickedness") is totally undefined.

(c) In I and II, the punishment is expulsion or exclusion, in I from the Garden of Eden, in II from the 'ādāmāh. In both cases the punishment should actually have been death; both times it is clearly in part the purpose of the narrative to single out the absence of this punishment as something unusual. The question remains whether the derivation of punishment from curse is also operative in this type of punishment, separation or exclusion.

In I we also find particular punishments imposed on the man, the woman, and the serpent, in which specific debilities are declared to be God's punishment. It is easy to hypothesize an earlier stage of the narrative in which it led up to just one punishment, expulsion. In III, the punishment is limitation of human lifespan, which plainly stands on the same footing as the particular punishments in I. In V, too, the punishment is a limitation of the possibilities open to humans, in this case the possibility

---

33. Skinner (*Genesis*, p. 147) refers to Ezekiel 32:21–23, where the same word appears: "Ezekiel dwells on their haughty violence and warlike prowess, and plainly intimates that for their crimes they were consigned to Sheol, where, however, they enjoy a kind of aristocratic dignity among the shades." As a distant parallel he cites a reference in the Koran (p. 140): "The Ḳoran has frequent references to the peoples of 'Ad and Thamûd, primaeval races noted for their giant stature and their daring impiety, to whom were attributed the erection of lofty buildings and the excavation of rock-dwellings, and who were believed to have been destroyed by a divine judgment (Sur. vii, xxvi, xli, xlvi, lxxxix)."

of a self-created unity, which would mean a transgression of the limitations imposed on the growth of human power.

Only in IV is the punishment annihilation. But the goal of the narrative is not the annihilation of humankind as such, but (a) the deliverance of a single individual from destruction, and (b) God's self-imposed limitation in his promise never to bring about such a catastrophe again.

(d) It is very striking that the final punishment is usually exclusion or separation rather than death and annihilation. In a similar vein, *all* these crime/punishment narratives contain some feature exhibiting something like pardon or amnesty. In I, the death that is threatened does not occur; the pardon is given its particular expression in verse 21, where God makes garments for the man and his wife. In II, it is the mark that protects the murderer from being murdered. In III, it is likewise the sparing of those who had transgressed their limits; the punishment consists *only* in a shortening of their lifespan. The situation is very similar in V, where the storming of heaven is punished not with annihilation but with the establshment of a limit.

Something totally new appears in IV: on the one hand, the merciless annihilation of humankind; on the other, the sparing of a single individual, which now takes on the character of deliverance from a catastrophe. At the same time, the annihilation of humankind is restricted to a single primordial catastrophe. In some of its features, the narrative of the destruction of Sodom and Gomorrah (Genesis 18—19) resembles the narrative of the deluge. By genre it belongs more with the narrative of the primal history than with the patriarchal stories.

(e) It is clear that the real conclusion of the primal history comes more after chapters 6—9 than in chapter 11.[34]

In the context of the deluge story the transition from primal

34. This position is now supported by R. Rendtorff, "Genesis 8,21 und die Urgeschichte des Jahwisten," *Kerygma und Dogma* 7 (1961): 69–78 (reprinted in his *Gesammelte Studien zum Alten Testament*, Theologische Bücherei 57 [München: Kaiser, 1975], pp. 188–97); see page 75: "Thus Genesis 8:21 constitutes the conclusion of the Yahwist's primal history."

history to history is clearly marked. The act of punishment, which by origin and nature is within the provenance of God alone because God is judge, is now delegated to humanity—at least within certain limits. For P, this takes place in 9:5–6, in the fundamental ordinance given to people after the deluge, making human life sacrosanct and giving *humans* the commandment to kill the murderer: the introduction of the death penalty, which is to be executed by humans.

For J, this takes place less openly; it is only hinted at in the crime/punishment narrative 9:20–27 (VI), in which for the first time in the Bible one individual pronounces a curse upon another. But this curse (9:24–25) functions as a punishment; it is the consequence of a transgression (9:22) and punishes a misdeed.

SUMMARY

If we examine the structure and primary motifs in the narratives of Genesis 1—11, it becomes clear that they are in fact dominated by the crime/punishment motif which shapes the narrative. The response to the question as to the reason for the exigencies, catastrophes, and shortcomings of human life, which is always the same here in its basic features, furnished the architectural skeleton for all these narratives. They are etiological narratives, in that they all derive from such questions and give their answer in narrative form. In them the etiological line coincides with the line of the tension that leads from transgression to punishment—but in such a way that the execution of the punishment involves simultaneously a merciful limitation of the punishment. This is the real axis of the narratives in Genesis 1—11.

At the beginning of this section I pointed out that there is no real Hebrew equivalent for "punishment."[35] This creates a difficulty. How God acts in these narratives should be defined more

35. Note that the semantic range of *dāraš* approximates our "punish"; see C. Westermann, "Die Verben des Fragens und Suchens im Alten Testament," *Kerygma und Dogma* 6 (1960): 2ff.

precisely. It might be asked whether the form of the crime/ punishment narratives in Genesis 1—11 serves to express a special way God deals with humankind, to the extent that they represent God essentially as the one who punishes or restrains evildoers, but spares their lives even as he does so. This would stand in sharp contrast to the Sumero-Babylonian myths in which the gods are basically the ones who determine human fate. This might be associated with the fact that in Mesopotamia the gods themselves have their own fates, whereas the God of the Old Testament does not. Seen in this light, could the narratives of the primal history be understood as a conscious countertype to the myths of the ancient Near East?

It might also be asked whether the Greek drama of fate does not also have this conception as its background; here, too, in Greek mythology, the gods have their fates and are subject to heimarmenē. It could be that this is why in Greek tragedy the crime/punishment nexus as such is still subject to heimarmenē: the guilt incurred through crime is understood as fate. This is fundamentally different from Genesis 1—11, where the crime/ punishment nexus is subject only to the Creator as Lord, who protects his creation by imposing limits as punishment.

In this sphere of inquiry many questions remain. In any case, the narratives in Genesis 1—11 must have been viewed against a very broad background.

IV
The Abraham Cycle
(12—25)

If initially we review this section simply for its narrative content, we notice at once that the narratives focus in strangely monotonous fashion on birth and death. In this respect they come surprisingly close to the genealogy of chapter 5. The tensions that give rise to the overwhelming majority of these narratives are tensions involving life and death. In the first narrative (12:10–20), the tension begins when Abraham says to Sarah that he is afraid: "They will kill me." In the promise narratives and the Hagar narratives, the concern is the birth of a child; in 18—19 it is destruction, death, and preservation. In 20, God says to Abimelech in a dream, "You shall surely die." Abraham acts as intercessor, praying that Abimelech's wife may once more bear children. The central point of the narrative is the birth of Isaac. In the Hagar narrative, we are told how she and her child are preserved from death. In 22, Abraham is commanded by God to sacrifice his child, who is then preserved from death. Additional births follow in 22:20ff. Chapter 23 tells of Sarah's death and burial. The final section, 25:1–11, reports the birth of additional children and the death of Abraham.

Closely allied to this observation is another: nowhere else in the Bible do we find mother and child as often as here. Indeed in the foreground stands the father and the relationship of the father to his child (15, 22). But it is possible that at an earlier stage the mother played a larger role in these stories. This is suggested by a series of observations. In the majority of the stories, the focus is on the mother. Often, as in chapter 18, we hear echoes of an earlier form in which the promise of a child was addressed to the mother. Here we have probably hit upon a very ancient stage of the family narrative. Undoubtedly the dominance of these motifs—birth and death, children and parents—suggests an important cycle of narratives whose origins go back to the earliest days of the Israelite people.

ORGANIZATION OF THE STORIES

An initial attempt to survey the various types of presentation reveals a surprising organization that cannot simply be written off as accidental. If the Abraham stories are given a preliminary gross classification according to the most conspicuous forms of presentation—narratives, promises, accounts of journeys, genealogies—they fall into three or four clearly recognizable groups. The promises recorded in narratives appear together as a conspicuous group in chapters 15—18. The journey accounts are grouped together in 12—13; later we find only 21:33–34 (apart from isolated statements like 20:1 and 22:19b). Chapters 16—24 contain only complete narratives; in 16 and 18 this complex is joined with the promise narratives. Outside of 16—24 we find narratives only in 12:10–20, which is included with the journey accounts as the story of Abraham's journey to Egypt, and in 13:5–13, which likewise belongs with the journey accounts in a wider sense. Genealogical information appears almost exclusively at the beginning and the end: 11:27–32 (JP); 22:20–24; (23 and 24); 25:1–6 (J), 7–11 (P), 12–18 (PJ). The narratives in 23 and 24 are based on brief genealogical statements.

A second arrangement cuts across this one, but still represents a preliterary organization of the narratives in the Abraham cycle. It was recognized by Gunkel (among others) and can easily be seen in the structure of the Abraham/Lot narratives.

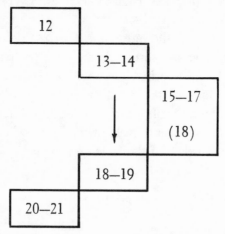

They surround the promise narratives (15—17 [18]) and interrupt the narratives that run from the peril of the mother to the birth of the son. Initially, it is only important to note that here, too, the preliterary arrangement includes an organization of the narratives according to their subject matter: the Lot narratives deal with territory. None of the other Abraham narratives is based on this motif. Furthermore, only in this interlude do we find types of narrative included in the Abraham cycle that are actually foreign to it: the war of the kings in chapter 14 and the destruction of the cities in chapter 19, the latter a narrative that with regard to its genre belongs more with the primal history than with the patriarchal history.

This second organization furthermore confirms the fact that the promise narratives in 15—17 (18) constitute a group. This much at least we can safely say in the light of these observations: the types of presentation and the types of narrative play a part as such in the development of the Abraham cycle. During the stages preceding the literary recensions of the cycle, these types were clearly perceived and must therefore have a significance for the early stages of development of this narrative cycle, which we shall now investigate in more detail.

FAMILY STORIES

The basic corpus of narratives in the Abraham cycle comprises family stories. The most important group of these deals with the fate of the matriarch and her child.[36] This group includes

15:1–6   Promise of a son and many descendants (17:1–27)
18:1–16 and 21:1–7   Announcement and birth of Isaac
12:10–20 Peril and preservation of the mother
20:1–18   Peril and preservation of the mother (compare verse 26)
16:1–16   Birth and peril of Hagar's son
21:8–21   Expulsion and preservation of Hagar's son

36. It is quite remarkable that we do not find a group of true Abraham stories, that is, stories in which Abraham really is the focus of events (a point also made by Noth, who arrives at this observation by a different route). When there is a dramatic concentration of the narrative in the Abraham cycle, Abraham is not really central; he may be a spectator or participant, but he is neither the subject nor object of crucial events. The Abraham cycle contains many narratives in which someone is threatened or endangered—but it is never Abraham.

The secondary line includes

19:30-38 Lot's daughters (origin of Moab and Ammon)
24.   Isaac's bride, the next matriarch
23.   Death and burial of the matriarch

Numerous as these texts are, the group comprises only a few independent narratives: 12, with its parallels in 20 and 26; 18:1-16 with 21:1-7; and 16, with its parallel in 21. Chapters 15 and 18 (together with 16) coincide with promise narratives.

18:1-16. The promise of a son in response to the exigency of childlessness is a motif frequently encountered in the realm of family narratives. Here—and only here—does the circle of the promise narrative coincide completely with the circle of the family narrative. Here, therefore, we have the crucial starting point for the transformation of a cycle of family sagas into a saga cycle defined by the promise to Abraham.

All exegetes have seen that 18:1-16 has been artfully combined with 18:17-33 and 19:1-29 (together with 30-38) to form a single entity, an intermediate narrative cycle. It was originally a separate narrative, the announcement of the birth of a child to a childless couple. This is a fixed and easily recognizable narrative motif throughout the Old Testament (it appears also, for example, in Ps. 113:9, in the context of praise), and it returns again in Luke 1. It constitutes one of the most typical family narratives. In Genesis 18 it has been substantially altered, but the ancient form can still be recognized rather easily from the many parallel developments the motif underwent.

I. The introductory clause "And Yahweh appeared to him" is a later introduction, defining the theme (like 22:1). In an earlier form, the narrative began with the surprising appearance of the three men, possibly preceded by a transitional statement defining the situation, like 11:30: "But Sarai was barren."

II. The original initial situation has been heightened in the present recension by the great age of Abraham and Sarah. In fact this is a totally different situation found in other stories (see

Gunkel, *Genesis*, HAT 1, no. 1, 7th ed. [Göttingen: Vandenhoeck & Kuprecht, 1966 ([1]1902)]). While constructing the Abraham cycle, the Yahwist introduced the motif "delay of the promise," which plays an important role in Exodus in a totally different setting.

III. In most of the narratives involving this motif, the messenger comes to the woman; the birth of the child was promised to her. This was probably true also in an earlier form of Genesis 18, as can still clearly be seen (in Judg. 13:3ff., a similar narrative, the angel also comes to the woman). What takes place here actually involves the messenger(s) and Sarah; Abraham remains wholly in the background and totally passive.

IV. In its present form 18:1–16 is the opening scene of a larger whole. This is probably why the birth of the promised child is not mentioned until a later passage. To judge from the parallels, in an earlier form the narrative itself contained the resolution of the tension developed in it; see the J verses from 21:1–7 containing the birth and naming of the child. Only with these verses do we have the inclusive whole of tension and resolution. The subject of the narrative is accordingly the archetypal distress of the woman in ancient times, childlessness, resolved by the announcement of a child through a divine messenger and the fulfillment of the message. This is the event for which God is praised in the Psalms. "He gives the barren woman a home, making her the joyous mother of children" (Ps. 113:9).

V. This narrative describes an archetypal experience of distress and its alleviation through God's miraculous intervention. It remains totally within the realm of the family; be it noted, however, that this is here the realm of crucial events. It has the same significance that deliverance from pursuit through God's miraculous intervention had for the nomadic group. Because of this significance it was recounted and handed down. Here we find the reality and tradition of deliverance, liberation, and redemption in the full theological sense of the word.

12:10(9)–20; 20:1–18; 26.[37] The narrative about the peril of the ancestress or matriarch, appearing in three variants, exhibits a type of narrative typical of the Abraham cycle. Here the starting point that produces the tension is a famine (in 12 and 26; not stated in 20). At the conclusion, Abraham (Isaac) is rich in possessions; in the middle stands the saving intervention of God. The uniqueness of the narrative, however, rests in a special complication: the famine forces the father to migrate to a foreign land (with a settled civilization), where a new peril is encountered, namely, the peril of the woman at the hands of the foreign ruler. It is nothing less than the peril of the mother of the clan.

The three variants in their amazing variety show how productive this narrative was in the early period and how much it was worked on. It is striking to note once more that in all three variants the subject is the wife, the mother. Even though this fact has been distorted in the forms that have been preserved, so that Abraham comes increasingly into the foreground, there is no escaping the impression that the story really is about the peril of the mother. "God delivers the woman who is to be the ancestress of Israel" (von Rad).

We can see where the real interest of this narrative is rooted when we compare it with Genesis 18. There it is a "natural" peril that endangers the woman in her life as wife and mother; here it is a "historical" peril, or, more simply, a peril at human hands, at the hands of a powerful man in alien territory. In this narrative we have a deposit of the earliest experience of the "power" of God, which, reaching beyond the realm of the family, can

---

37. See C. A. Keller, "Die Gefährdung der Ahnfrau," ZAW 66 (1954): 181–91. Keller begins with a pointed description of the problems faced by study of the Old Testament narratives on the basis of motifs and literary types. He then uses Genesis 12, 20, and 26 as an example to show that these chapters were put together out of a basic motif "in which a man fears for his life on account of his beautiful wife and takes refuge in an unavoidable lie," and a series of quite diverse compositional motifs. In my opinion, this approach fails to recognize that in a narrative the totality is primary, the individual motifs secondary (Gunkel; Kaiser, *Das sprachliche Kunstwerk;* Jolles; and many others).

deliver and protect from alien power. This helps explain why the variants concentrate on this effect God has on the powerful foreigner. Not until the narrative was incorporated in the Abraham cycle was the reference to the mother and her promised son added.

Chapters 16 and 21, the Hagar Narratives. Once again the protagonists of these narratives are the women, the mothers. Once again the realm within which the events take place is the family. One strand in chapter 16 (see above) is a promise narrative of the same type as Genesis 18. It is interwoven with an etiological strand, itself composite (vv. 13 and 14). On the second part of the Hagar narrative in chapter 21, see above. It is a deliverance or preservation narrative interwoven with the motif of promised descendants.

Both narratives, 16 and 21, are closely allied in their first section, the quarrel between the women. This is a totally different motif, relatively independent in each instance from the second section of the narrative; it is quite possible that at one time it constituted an independent narrative. In both passages, 16 and 21, the description of the quarrel gives the impression that it was initially of utmost severity, but that the narrator ended up mitigating the quarrel (the role of Abraham).

In order to understand this quarrel motif and its narrative development, it must be noted particularly that in the Jacob cycle the rivalry between the two brothers is a major theme, whereas in the Abraham cycle the quarrel is fought between the women, the mothers. Such a quarrel is not mentioned again in this form, but it can still be recognized in abbreviated and allusive form in the interlude 29:31—30:24. A particular social constellation must be reflected here, in which this quarrel between the women was a fundamental form of strife.[38]

In the present form of the narratives in 16 and 21, it looks as

---

38. Something similar appears to be reflected in the Nuzi tablets; see G. Fohrer, "Tradition und Interpretation im Alten Testament," ZAW 73 (1961): 1–30, with additional bibliography.

though the quarrel between the women serves merely as an occasion for what is actually to be told, which then follows in the second section of each narrative. This displacement took place when the narrative, as part of the Abraham cycle, was made to focus on the promised son. Behind it stands an earlier form in which the quarrel had its own significance and determined the relative positions of wife and concubine as well as of their sons. We can no longer reconstruct this stage of the narrative, but the two variants of the quarrel exhibit an important difference that points in the right direction: 16 is concerned with the position or honor of the woman, 21 with the son's right of succession. Thus in their first sections 16 and 21 belong to a group of family narratives dealing with social struggles. Their unique feature is that the woman is the real protagonist.

19:30–38, Lot's Daughters. In contrast to all the previously discussed narratives of the Abraham cycle, 19:30–38 is not an independent narrative, developing a tension to its resolution. It is an appendix to the narrative of the destruction of the cities, with a clear etiological purpose. It recounts the origin of Moab and Ammon.

The initial situation is similar to that in 18: a woman (here the two sisters) cannot bear a child. Here, however, this situation does not issue in an event in which their distress is brought to a resolution. Instead, without any tension or complication, we are simply told how the sisters find their own solution, committing an act that would normally be an outrage, but in their desperate situation was a daring albeit profligate recourse. The narrative itself—and this is important—contains no trace of any judgment of this act, either positive or negative. It is like a newspaper story, a report of a curiosity; the etiology attached itself to this curiosity. But one positive feature links this curiosity with the Abraham cycle: it is a family story, and even in this highly unusual act the mothers retain their special significance for the family and its history, here the preservation of the family made possible by the action of the women. The episode takes on negative overtones in the composition as a whole, which implicitly suggests a contrast between the course of Lot's family history and that of Abraham.

Chapters 22, 23, and 24. All three chapters belong to other groups. But one clearly independent strand links each of them with this group: they, too, deal with the life and survival of the family. In chapter 22, the peril and preservation of the son is recounted alongside and together with a different incident. It is the narrator's extraordinary artistry that gives voice to this tension and its resolution while he is engaged in telling his own story, so that the subsidiary narrative strand has the effect of an independent story.

Chapters 23 and 24 each expand at length on a genealogical entry. They are related to the group of narratives discussed here in that they both deal with the matriarch and both develop around an important event in the life of the family. The significance of the matriarch is tacitly underlined in both chapters through a detailed description of how she became the wife of the patriarch, how she died, and how she was buried.

TERRITORIAL CONFLICT

13:5–13. Conflict between the herdsmen of Abraham and of Lot[39]

21:22–32. Conflict between the herdsmen of Abraham and of Abimelech

26:18–33. Isaac and Abimelech; conflict over territory and water

If we examine the form and structure of these three passages, we note first of all that in this group there are no narratives in the strict sense. The two Abraham narratives in 13 and 21 merely report the settlement of the dispute; the passages in 26 contain more allusions and fragments than real narratives.

39. See H. J. Boecker, *Redeformen des Rechtslebens im Alten Testament* (Wissenschaftliche Monographien zum Alten und Neuen Testament 14 [Neukirchen-Vluyn: Neukirchener Verlag, 1964]), p. 118, where this passage is cited as an instance of the mediation form.

How is this circumstance to be explained? In many cases the reports as they have been handed down contain only the conclusion of the conflict: Abraham yields and gives Lot his choice; Abraham makes a covenant with Abimelech; the well is named in commemoration of their oath, etc. When we attempt to start from this point and reconstruct the tension that is resolved in the conclusion, we see at once that the ancient narrative must have recounted more than the conflict and its outcome; there must also have been an initial situation giving rise to the conflict. This situation must have produced in each case the particular complication that issued in the conflict. The cause of the conflict could vary widely; in one case, for example, the narrative deals with groups that travel together (13), and in another with groups that meet at a well (26). A frequently recurring cause is the group's increase. The motive for the conflict lies in the fact that the increase, a result of God's blessing, is followed by a sense of constriction leading to friction. But we find nothing beyond general summary comments like 13:6: "The land could not support both of them dwelling together." We hear nothing of the concrete initial situations. Therefore we do not find literary tension and resolution.

In this cycle we are probably dealing with remnants of what was once a flourishing narrative cycle. All that are left are, for the most part, very general statements containing the facts and dates to which the narratives led up, such as the name of the well.

I would here cite Noth's explanation of how the Isaac stories in Genesis 26 came into being (*A History of Pentateuchal Traditions*, pp. 105f.):

> Next comes the theme, treated in several separate narratives, of the dispute with the old owners of the arable land over the possession, or alternatively the right of use, of the water places and specifically . . . of the groundwater wells. The theme itself had emerged out of the reality of daily relations; its exposition in detail, however, arose out of the intention to explain etiologically the names of several groups of groundwater wells (vv. 17, 19–23, 25b–33). . . .

On the whole, these Isaac stories give the impression of being even more original traditio-historically than the stories of the West Jordan Jacob. They stand, as a matter of fact, closer to the origin of the "patriarchal" tradition than do the latter. The scene of the Isaac stories was laid in the midst of the heavily settled arable land; hence in their case we stand on the boundary zone between the sphere of the settled inhabitants and the sphere of those migratory intruders who desired admission. The single theme of all the Isaac stories is the possession of arable land and the dispute with the older inhabitants of the land, especially over the most valued element of the arable land, the water.

I am in complete agreement with what Noth says here about the Isaac tradition in chapter 26, up to the point of what he says about the formation of this very ancient tradition. His statement that "its exposition in detail . . . arose out of the intention to explain etiologically the names of several groups of groundwater wells" seems dubious to me. Noth finds here the exposition in detail, but finds the actual theme in the dispute with the older inhabitants. This seems to me to indicate that the narratives as such are not merely etiologies but well-conflict narratives. The point of the narratives is not really the naming of the well but the outcome of the conflict, which is frequently echoed in the name given to the well. The naming is a secondary motif, not the point or nucleus of the narrative. It would be more accurate to say that the exposition in detail, that is, the origin and complication of the conflict, vanished in the course of transmission. We are left with only a remnant of these narratives, and it is not surprising that this remnant is limited for the most part to facts and dates.

When Noth indicates that the dispute with the inhabitants of the arable land is the only theme of the Isaac narratives in chapter 26, he confirms the observation that we have here within the Genesis narratives a grouping defined by subject matter and points to an especially clear example of such a grouping. The cycle of well-conflict narratives cannot be understood clearly until it is recognized that we are dealing here with "war" in a period before there was an organized state. What war was after the formation of the Israelite nation and what it meant for human life in this epoch are represented by the quarrel in its various forms. In this case we already find a conflict over territory and sustenance, two crucial causes of war after the development of the state. From the perspective of the Old Testament, we are dealing here with the preliminary stage of what we will encounter in the next stage (Joshua and Judges) as conflicts between the tribes.

We will encounter a different form of conflict in this early period in the Jacob/Laban stories.

Besides conflict between men, there was also conflict between women, like the one we found in the two Hagar narratives. While the conflict between men involves territory and sustenance, the subject of the conflict between women is position (in the social group) and honor; the former is in the realm of "foreign relations," the latter in the realm of "domestic relations."

This whole subject can only be touched on here and deserves further inquiry: where in the early narratives do we encounter the phenomenon of quarrel or conflict, what rhetorical form is it cast in by the narratives, how much can still be seen of the path that leads from quarrel to war, where and how in the later historical narratives and reports do we still find echoes of the prehistory of conflict, etc.

The phenomenon of conflict in its various forms, traces of which are still found in the early narratives of the Old Testament, is of course a universal phenomenon. But in the high civilizations surrounding Israel it is found likewise only in traces (for example, in the Gilgamesh Epic) which are in fact more fragmentary and scattered than in the Old Testament.[40]

40. It must therefore be asked whether Old Testament scholarship is not required at this point to make use of the science that deals with such phenomena of human society prior to the development of high civilization, namely ethnology. The same question is raised by a number of phenomena, traces of which are still found in the early strata of the Old Testament.

For a basic orientation I would refer the reader to A. Rüstow, *Ortsbestimmung der Gegenwart*, vol. 1: *Ursprung der Herrschaft* (Erlenbach: Rentsch, 1950), pages 25ff., an appendix to the Introduction on the significance of ethnology for

ACCOUNTS OF SUCCESS, CHAPTERS 23 AND 24

The three extended narratives contained in the Abraham cycle (chapters 22, 23, and 24) stand together at its conclusion. This arrangement, too, should be considered deliberate. Of the three, 23 and 24 constitute a group, in that they are both accounts that have developed out of genealogical notices, although they differ completely in style (see p. 65 above).

It must be emphasized at the outset that in these descriptive narratives we have a totally different type of narrative from, say, the narrative of Genesis 12:1–20. They lack the element that makes a literary narrative, namely tension that is brought to a resolution. It may be objected that the two stories do in fact contain tension: Abraham's commission to his steward raises the question of whether the enterprise will succeed. Abraham's plan to acquire a burial place on the death of his wife generates tension: will he succeed? The claim is possible, and it is possible to find the description of events in both narratives such that the listener or reader awaits the outcome with suspense. But this tension is of a totally different kind; it does not grow out of the sequence of events, but is engendered artificially. Herein lies the real disparity between this type of narrative and the older, simpler type, not in the richness of detail as such, as is often asserted. Here, to borrow a term from Jolles, we are dealing with a different kind of intellectual occupation. A sociological and intellectual change must have taken place making it possible for the old, simple, and yet action-packed narratives to be superseded by these narratives, which involve little action but compensate by being all the more vivid and "lovely." With respect to Genesis 24, one could say that the function of narration itself has

---

the study of history. In a few brief lines, Rüstow draws attention to the path leading from ethnology to the science of history. There is a striking parallel to Old Testament studies: in ethnology, too, the uniform evolution that dominated the great works of the nineteenth century (for example, Frazer) was countered by an opposing antievolutionism. Rüstow goes on to indicate the limitations of these "highly deserving heroes who slew the evil dragon of evolutionism."

changed. Formerly the narrative existed for the sake of its content, that is, the sequence of events recorded in the narrative. Now we find a form of presentation in which the emphasis has shifted from the events described to the description itself—what we might cautiously call literature.

If we go back to the actual events recorded in Genesis 24, we are still left with a genealogical report: Abraham sent for a distant relative, Rebecca, to be the wife of his son Isaac.[41] This passing remark has been developed literarily into a large and colorful product. In the course of this elaboration it has also been given a pronounced theological stamp as a narrative illustrating God's guidance. But it is far removed from the truly theological narrative in chapter 22, in that God's action in 24 is as straightforward and unproblematical as the description of the events itself.[42]

That Genesis 24 remains wholly in the realm of family narrative has already been stated.

23:1–20. Here, too, we have a simple and straightforward event elaborated at length. The account has been interpolated in P within a brief notice of Sarah's death and burial. The extremely vivid description of the purchase seems strange in P. We may assume that it is based on an earlier version, but what were its context and purpose? The really unusual aspect of this account is that what the style of the patriarchal narratives elsewhere would have stated in a single sentence is developed at length into an independent entity. It is possible that the account simply came into being in a preliminary stage of P out of a desire to elaborate on the acquisition of this sepulchre of the matriarch so as to lend heightened significance to this act. This possibility is supported

41. See Gunkel's commentary, page 248: "The subject matter here is so slight that it would not suffice for an ancient 'saga.' Neither are there any real 'complications.' The narrator therefore could hardly have had more than a 'note' about Isaac's marriage, which he elaborated so lovingly."

42. It remains to inquire into the relationship between these "success stories" and the promise of God's present aid ("I will be with you"; see above), for they tell how God's presence manifests itself effectually.

by the almost refrainlike repetition of the sentence "Bury your dead" in the conversation, as well as the fact that for P burial is not a sacral act, and the secular act of purchasing a tomb might underscore this. But it is also possible to suggest that P has here "legalized" a narrative that had formerly recounted the acquisition of Machpelah in a totally different form, namely as a conflict narrative. This suggestion is supported by the independent emphasis still discernible on the side of the "Hittites," as well as by certain parallels in Hittite legal texts that make it very likely that behind Genesis 23 there is a very ancient narrative reflecting pre-Israelite legal practice.[43]

THEOLOGICAL NARRATIVES

22:1–19.   God tempts Abraham

18:17–33.   Announcement of destruction and Abraham's question

12:1–3.   Command and promise to Abraham

15:1–6.   Promise of success to Abraham

Plus the secondary promise narratives

Genesis 22. In its present form, the meaning and purpose of the narrative lies in the testing of Abraham, as the first sentence states and as the words of the angel later indicate: "For now I know. . . ." Von Rad in particular has shown in his analysis how a whole series of earlier strata can be recognized behind this final form. One of these earlier forms is thought by many exegetes to have been a cult etiology explaining the name of the mountain of sacrifice. Here, too, this etiology seems to me to be an important feature, but not the actual purpose of an earlier form of the narrative in which all the emphasis had not yet been shifted to the testing of Abraham. Another etiological feature, probably

---

43. M. R. Lehmann, "Abraham's Purchase of Machpelah and Hittite Law," *BASOR* 129 (1953): 15–18.

even earlier but perhaps connected with the first, was the explanation of how the sacrifice of the firstborn came to be commuted to an animal sacrifice, which is also attested in the Covenant Code. The nucleus of the earlier form of the narrative, however, seems to me to have been the deliverance of the son who was destined to be sacrificed, a statement that can be supported only by a detailed exegesis. This earlier form would then be closely related to the preservation of Hagar's child in chapter 21.

All the more closely does the narrative in its present form differ from the earlier narratives. This form is based quite clearly on intellectual theological reflection, on the explicitly theological concept of *nissāh*, testing. This concept, placed thematically at the beginning of the narrative, points beyond the two simple basic modes of experiencing God's activity—the experience of his favor in deliverance and preservation, of his rejection in defeat and disaster—to a third possibility: the experience of disaster can be the result of something other than God's rejection in wrath; it can be based on God's purpose to test a man. This possibility is represented in a narrative; Genesis 22 is narrative theology. Here narrative has taken on a new and different function: the framing of theological questions and statements. It is clear that this function does not belong to the earliest stratum in the formation of the Genesis narratives, but to a later stage.

18:17–32. This passage contains God's conversation with Abraham, the announcement of the destruction of the cities, and Abraham's question. In contrast to Genesis 22, it is not based on an ancient narrative. Most exegetes describe it as a conversation growing out of reflection on the question put to God by Abraham in the narrative. There is great difference of opinion whether it is a fresh composition by the Yahwist (von Rad, Noth, and others) or a much later composition from the prophetic period. In any event the conception of this conversation falls within a tradition context in which questions like the one discussed here could be answered by a narrative. This means it would be necessary to survey and examine all the narratives and narrative fragments in the Old Testament in which the narrative performs this function of presenting theological questions.

In my opinion, Genesis 18:17–32 represents an expanded announcement of judgment, not against Israel but against others, like the oracles against the nations. It is certainly older than eighth- and seventh-century prophecy. The motif appears again in Genesis 6—9: here, too, the deluge is announced in advance, and to the one who will *not* be subject to judgment.[44] The distinctive element here in contrast to 6—9 is the "intercession" of Abraham. Its great importance must go back to an early date: the motif appears several times in the patriarchal history in quite different contexts. These elements—announcement of judgment and intercession—have been expanded by being placed in something resembling a problem narrative, a theological narrative. As such it resembles Genesis 22, but it differs markedly in realization. There are no later examples. It is quite striking that such theological narratives appear only in the Abraham cycle. May we explain this fact by suggesting that the final redactors of the patriarchal stories, J and E, found it possible to frame such narratives within the Abraham cycle precisely because it was the most fluid element in the traditional material they had before them?

Closely resembling the theological narratives are the texts in which the subject matter is the giving of a promise to Abraham, the secondary promise narratives. But this narrative configuration of the promise motif must be distinguished clearly from the theological narratives proper. These are not true narratives but rather interpolations of the promise motif, now used to bind the patriarchal stories together and at the same time linking them with the total structure of the Pentateuch. This motif, too, is given narrative form; but these narratives, such as Genesis 12:1–3; 15:1–6; or 22:15–18, belong to the stage when the stories of the patriarchs were being fused and assembled.

---

44. That God warns his people of dangers threatening them is a particularly characteristic feature of the "religion of the patriarchs."

GENESIS 19 AND 14

The destruction of the cities is a narrative that became associated with the Abraham cycle at an early date. With respect to its genre, it belongs more to the primal history than the patriarchal history. Its point is not really the destruction of the cities as such, but the escape of Lot and his family.

Genesis 14 is a very late addition to the Abraham cycle. It is a narrative that has nothing more in common with the patriarchal stories than the names Abraham and Lot. Its genre is so totally different that it must be examined separately from the other patriarchal narratives.

V

The Jacob—Esau Cycle

(25—36)

GENERAL FEATURES

There are a series of differences between the cycle of Jacob/Esau narratives and that of the Abraham narratives, which can only be accounted for by the assumption that the two cycles were handed down independently during part of their history.

(a) With respect to the promises, one is immediately struck by the fact that real promise *narratives* (primary and secondary) are found only in the Abraham cycle. After chapter 25 there are no more promise narratives; the promise texts that do occur all have the nature of interpolations, additions, or brief notices.

What does this observation mean? J and E (and P after them) associated the promises essentially with Abraham. The explanation that this is because Abraham was the first of the patriarchs will not suffice. Instead J and E found in the existing Abraham cycle the starting point for their more extended and comprehensive promise motif in the more narrow and limited promise motif that dominates the narrative(s) of the promise of the birth of a son. Starting from this point, a group of promise narratives (15—18) took shape within the Abraham cycle such as could not arise elsewhere. We must therefore conclude that the promise motif is associated with the Abraham cycle in a different and more emphatic way than with the other narrative cycles of the patriarchal history.

(b) It was stated of the Abraham narratives at the outset that they focus in a strangely monotonous way on birth and death, and that here mother (or parents) and child are often the center of interest. Neither observation is true at all of the Jacob/Esau narratives. Other social relationships are in the foreground here, primarily the relationship of brother to brother. But there is also a whole series of differentiated relationships and events, all of which either do not appear or appear only peripherally in 12—25. The monotony of birth and death, the concentration on the single great question and concern of whether the family will perpetuate itself in a son takes a backseat in 25—36 to other differentiated questions.

(c) In the Abraham narrative, everything institutional, both secular and sacred, is remarkably de-emphasized. Even when sanctuaries appear, when altars and the like are mentioned, they have scarcely any function of their own. The statements about them are vague and general. The situation in 25—36 is clearly and unmistakably different. In this portion of the patriarchal history, institutions, sacred places, sacred acts, covenants, legal definitions begin to take on an importance that cannot be separated from the narratives. Here, too, we find an unmistakable difference in this cycle.

STRUCTURE

As we go from chapter 25 through 36, we cannot help noticing that, here, too, there is a kind of arrangement by subject matter.

If we use the gross classification described above (pp. 57f.), we can recognize two groups, since the promise narratives are excluded. The large section 25:21—33:16 contains almost exclusively narratives. With 33:17 we come to reports of journeys, which, together with genealogical notices, extend from 33:17 through 36, again almost without exception. For the first group (25:21—33:16), it is important to note that chapters 29—31, although comprising individual narratives, constitute a fixed composition, thus differing clearly from the individual narratives preceding (25:21—28:22) and following (32:1—33:16).

How can these narratives be grouped internally? We find four narrative cycles, three of which are cohesive; the fourth consists of passages scattered throughout the whole: (1) Jacob and Esau, birth and firstborn (25:21—28:9); (2) Jacob and Esau, return (32—33); (3) Jacob and Laban (29—31); (4) sanctuary narratives.

We shall first examine these cycles independently and then inquire into their mutual relationship. The first narratives are determinative for the entire cycle: the birth of two sons (25:21—26a) initiates the sequence of events that runs through the entire section. Chapters 25—28, like 32—33, are concerned with the relationship between these two brothers. Here we have the clearest difference from the Abraham stories, which were concerned primarily with the sequence of generations, a vertical line. Chapters 25—28 and 32—33 are concerned with the horizontal line of the relationship between two brothers. In the four units that in 25—28 constitute the Jacob/Esau cycle in the narrower sense and in the whole of 32—33 (except for 32:1–3), the action is concentrated on what takes place between these two. This alone makes for a greater material uniformity in the Jacob/Esau cycle than in the Abraham cycle.

CHAPTERS 25—28

The most striking narrative in 25—28, and the most important for the cycle, is 27:1–45, the story of Jacob's deception to obtain the blessing of the firstborn. Formally, the size of narrative should be emphasized. It would be incorrect to speak of its "scale"; what we are dealing with is not an extensively developed description of a straightforward sequence of events as in Genesis 24, but the very dense depiction of a series of events so complex that it demands such length. None of the narratives in 12—25 deals with such a complex episode. There are two precisely parallel actions: the blessing of Jacob (vv. 1–29) and the blessing of Esau (vv. 30–40), with a conclusion (vv. 41–45) that tells the outcome of the deception for the family and for the two brothers —Esau's attack on Jacob and Jacob's flight.

If we now look for the arch of tension that holds this series of events together, the difference between this narrative and those of the Abraham cycle comes into even sharper focus. The tension does not arise from a given situation such as a famine or the barrenness of a woman, but from a human act that intervenes in the regular course of events. This receives almost classical expression in Genesis 27.

The regular course of events altered by human action here involves a blessing ceremony.[45] This is the first instance of such a blessing in the patriarchal history, and it determines the structure of the narrative in chapter 27. The blessing of a son by his father, who is dying or near death, is here presupposed as a ritual act, closely defined in every detail, the course of which is minutely described by the narrative. It is something like a precultic ritual, a ritual belonging to the realm of the family and highly significant within it, consisting of the following acts:

    I. Summons of the father (or request of the son)
    II. Identification (or naming) of the one to be blessed
    III. Offering of food and drink, nourishment for the father

45. It is quite striking that blessings play no role at all in Genesis 12—25, and that there is no narrative in which Abraham blesses his son Isaac (or any other). Is this because J's literary shaping of the Abraham narratives was so dominated by his newly coined concept of blessing (blessing as promise; see above), and especially by 12:1–3, that the earlier blessing of the son by his father receded into the background?

IV. Approach of the son to kiss the father (touching)

V. Pronouncing of the blessing

Rebecca intervenes in this fixed and regular ritual by countering the summons of the father (I) with her own summons to Jacob, intending deceit, thus producing deception in the act of identification (II). The subsequent acts of the ritual proceed normally.

The climax of the tension that begins with Rebecca's intervention now lies in the second repetition of the ritual, at precisely the same point, the identification of the son to be blessed (II). Now the regular course of events explodes in the horror of the father and the outcry of the son who has been cheated of his blessing. Esau's lament is followed by his plea for a blessing, and in the fifth act the two sequences converge once more; a blessing is pronounced over Esau, too, but its words give Esau only a shattered blessing, actually reminiscent of the curse on Cain.

This analysis shows that the skeleton of the narrative is the blessing ritual in its individual acts, culminating in the pronouncing of the blessing; in its reduplication it brings the tension to a climax and to an interim resolution. But the temporary nature of this resolution already hides the seeds of a new action, which receives exposition in the conclusion (vv. 41–45). Thus the narrative in chapter 27, despite its relative self-sufficiency, is nevertheless a part of a larger narrative whole.

How are the other narratives contained in 25—28 related to this nucleus?

25:27–34 (J), the pottage of lentils. As is generally stated, this episode is a parallel to 27, but it is a different kind of narrative. Materially, the most important difference is that totally different institutions are involved: in 27 a blessing, in 25:27–34 the right of primogeniture (*bᵉkōrāh*). The two were originally independent (as can still be seen from the secondary addition 27:36, which links the two stories) and point to two different stages of family law.

Formally, 25:27–34 is not a true narrative; it does not carry the weight of a story that moves from tension to its resolution. It is rather a mere episode or anecdote in the sense of a joke. It is told to make people laugh. What evokes laughter is the disproportion in the transaction that is concluded, caused by the doltish greed of one who sells his birthright.

In addition, this joke plays off the clever herdsman against the uncouth hunter. Here, however, the narrative leaves the realm of family narrative and enters a broader domain, in which various occupations coexist or compete (see Noth, *A History of Penta-teuchal Traditions*, pp. 96f.). It is this particular feature that explains how such a joke came to be incorporated in the Jacob/Esau cycle, where it is certainly out of place on the basis of its narrative form. The rivalry between the brothers, which is the subject of the whole narrative cycle, extends beyond the realm of the family to the competition between two different ways of life, which is the particular point of this narrative.

The artistry of the composition reveals itself here in another feature: an anecdote or joke is set by its very nature within an intimate framework. The interpolated joke here furnishes a tiny vignette of everyday life, a scene reminiscent of a picture by Brueghel. But this narrative genre goes strikingly well with the narrative of chapter 27, even though the latter has a totally different format. The blessing ritual runs its course within the most intimate sphere of family life, and its elements include the nourishing food the father receives. In this feature the anecdote about the pottage goes well with the great narrative of chapter 27.

25:21–26a (J), birth of Jacob and Esau. This section belongs to the group of genealogical notices that have been expanded in the direction of becoming narratives. Two totally different birth stories have been interwoven.

I. Verse 21.   Isaac's intercession for his barren wife Rebecca
    24–26a. Birth and naming of the twins

The motif of the barren wife furnishes the basis here as it does in Genesis 18, but with a different twist. The promise of a child through a divine messenger is replaced by a human action (as in chapter 27), the intercession of the patriarch. The difference from the Abraham narratives is striking: in the same situation, Abraham can only lament helplessly! The vouchsafing of a child is associated with human intercession, to which Yahweh accedes. The story is something like a precursor of 1 Samuel 1, except that no priest is involved; the father is the intercessor. As in the blessing ceremony, we have something like a precultic ritual. Verses 24–26a can follow verse 21 directly; the promise is followed by its fulfillment; the children are born and given names.

The simple narrative of the birth and naming of the brothers does not contain anything about their rivalry, but it sets the stage. It is hinted at obliquely in the minor feature of Jacob's holding Esau's heel. Through its association with verses 22–23, this narrative furnishes the prelude to the narrative cycle of the rivalry between the two brothers. Verse 21 could be a remnant, the reduction of a narrative to a mere notice, for the tension is never developed. This reduction might have taken place when the passage was linked with verses 22–23, to which it now serves as an introduction.

II. Verse 22a. Lament of pregnant Rebecca
      b. Rebecca's inquiry of Yahweh
      23. God's answer, the tribal saying

This is an independent, self-sufficient episode. The statement "So she went to inquire of Yahweh" can only mean that she went to a sanctuary, and in fact a sanctuary of Yahweh. Here, then, we very obviously have a cultic action from a later period: inquiry of God when faced with personal distress in order to receive a favorable oracle has been projected into the patriarchal period. The response, too, points beyond family narrative; it is a tribal saying in the form of a typical oracle, in which the struggling of the children in their mother's womb is interpreted. In content, the response leads up to a statement indicating which of two tribes will dominate. This is no longer family history, but tribal history.

27:46 and 28:1-9 (P), the wives of Esau and Jacob. This P narrative illustrates how powerful was the continuing influence of the basic motif, fraternal rivalry. Despite all the radical changes undertaken by P, this section is still determined by the contrast between the two brothers. The initiative of their mother likewise reappears, as in 27; in addition, the P narrative retained the old motif of Rebecca's lament, although placing it in a totally different context. P's own contribution is less important for us here than his testimony to the survival of the most important narrative motifs with extensive possibilities for variation.

CHAPTERS 32—33, JACOB'S RETURN

This section is closely associated with 25—28 (especially chapter 27), even though in its present context it follows 29—31 directly. It is a single narrative, interrupted only by the encounter with God at Peniel. Thus within the totality of the Jacob/Esau cycle we can distinguish two great complexes that are linked together: 27 and 32—33, coupled with 29—31.

Chapters 32—33 are a complex and imposing composition. They constitute a narrative in the strict sense, because the structure is clearly determined by a single tension: as Jacob returns, he learns that his brother is approaching with four hundred men. What will be the outcome?

The narrative does, however, clearly transcend the limits of a family narrative, and that in two respects.

I. We find here once again the peculiarity of the Jacob/Esau stories that the tensions are not limited to the realm of the elemental (famine, barrenness) and personal (conflict between women, deliverance of a child) but include institutional factors. This is accomplished with great artistry in Genesis 32—33. I will single out just one point: the encounter described here has been remarkably ceremonialized. It proceeds like a public ceremony with fixed protocol. It is not improbable that the narrator is picturing in his mind a familiar court ritual and has shaped the episode accordingly. In one passage (33:3) such a ritual even comes through in the very words used: the Amarna letters contain the formula "Before the feet of my lord I bow, seven times and seven." It is easy to imagine the entire event down to the last detail taking place between a sovereign and his vassal, who is seeking reconciliation with his lord on account of some transgression. The narrative would then describe the submission of a vassal, in which the tension is resolved. It is a surprising resolution. The encounter that Jacob so fears is in fact resolved favorably: the brothers are reconciled. But this reconciliation involves Jacob's submission, a submission that he almost forces on his brother.

II. In this resolution we find the key to another unique feature of this narrative: it is also a theological narrative of great profundity. It includes an interpretation of the relationship between blessing and mercy that attests profound theological reflection. This aspect of the narrative cannot be examined in detail here. A suggestion must suffice: the narrator guides the rivalry between the brothers over their blessing to the conclusion that the one who received the blessing falls at the feet of his unblessed brother![46]

CHAPTERS 29—31, JACOB AND LABAN

In 29—31 it is possible to find relatively independent units such as the compact with Laban or the separate collection 29:31—30:24 (the birth and naming of the children). The chapters nevertheless constitute a single coherent narrative. It differs

46. Chapter 33 is a "theological narrative" in a totally different sense than chapter 22. The latter takes a theological concept ("God tested . . .") as its starting point and is organized around theological concepts. In chapter 33, on the contrary, the theological reflection has been worked into the events of the story in such a way that no theological concepts are needed.

from all the previous narratives in Genesis by virtue of the fact that a period of many years, from the arrival at the well in 29:1ff. to Laban's return in 32:1, is encompassed in a single narrative. This also sets 29—31 apart from the framework in which it is placed. Chapters 27 and 32—33 are also detailed and differentiated narratives; but in both it is a single self-contained event that is narrated, whereas in 29—31 it is a series of events stretching over several years. In this respect (and in many others) 29—31 resembles the Joseph novella.

To summarize the narrative content of 29—31 as briefly as possible: we are told here how Jacob, having come to Laban as a powerless and penniless fugitive, departs from him as a great and rich man. The narrative describes the consequences of the blessing. A certain tension arises from the given situation: Jacob, seeking refuge from his brother, has to live with a stranger (albeit a relative) in a strange land. Can the blessing be efficacious in this setting? The resolution comes at the very end: the compact with Laban confirms Jacob's right to all he has acquired. But this conclusion also shows that the dominant motif in 29—31 is that of the conflict (just as the narratives of well conflicts often end with a compact). The special feature of this conflict is that, although Jacob is blessed, he comes powerless before Laban. Anything he gains through the power of the blessing can be taken away at once by his powerful host. Jacob must rely on wiles; the conflict is thus essentially intellectual. It is intensified almost to the point of violence; at the last moment, this is avoided by the compact.

This conclusion shows that the conflict here is already very close to what will replace it: battle and war. But the narrative still belongs to the epoch in which conflict takes the place of war; war is not yet possible. Yet 29—31 is clearly distinct from the earlier conflict narratives. The basis is still rivalry between two individuals living in the same place. But the quarrel does not remain in the realm of the elemental and personal; the situation is much more highly differentiated, and an institutional element appears—in 29–31, primarily legal institutions. And this observation applies not only to the concluding compact, described with all its formalities in verses 43–54, but also to 31:22–42, where the judicial process in case of theft or suspected theft has shaped the narrative in all its details.[47]

A further area not found in the earlier narratives is opened up by the servitude of Jacob, who performs labor outside his own clan that must be regulated by formal contract.[48] A series of possibilities and complications arising from such a contract are included in the narrative in 29 and 30.

Thus the Jacob/Laban narrative in 29–31 is a form of narrative on the very periphery of family narrative, at the point of transition to tribal and historical narrative. It illustrates impressively how the framework of family episode, the development of rivalry between relatives, is almost shattered by inclusion of institutions that suggest more extended social forms.[49]

ENCOUNTERS WITH GOD AND CULTIC OBSERVANCES

28:10–22. Bethel
32:2–3.   Mahanaim
32:23–33. Peniel
35:1–7.   Shechem/Bethel
35:14–15. Stone pillar and drink offering at Bethel

---

47. See the analysis of Genesis 31:25–42 in H. J. Boecker, *Redeformen des Rechtlebens im Alten Testament* (Neukirchen-Vluyn: Neukirchener Verlag, 1964), pp. 41–45.

48. The purpose of the contract is ultimately definition of boundaries followed by separation. The Abraham/Lot conflict also ends with (peaceful) separation and division of territory. But what a difference there is in the mode of presentation!

49. Noth (*A History of Pentateuchal Traditions*, pp. 91–94) outlines an earlier form of the Jacob/Laban narrative that in its pure development would be a prototype of war. The parties to this conflict are not nations or peoples but clans. Trickery is an important method of combat. As exemplified here by the trickery of Jacob, it is just as legitimate as the use of violence in war. But then the conception of this narrative must be located in a period when the latter was the normal form of war. Justification of Jacob's actions becomes necessary only at a stage when such robbery through trickery is no longer legitimate.

In this group of narratives Jacob alone is mentioned. The two brothers never appear together in them; Esau never experiences an appearance of God or participates in liturgical acts. This fact alone shows that we are dealing with an independent narrative cycle.

The difference from the Abraham stories is apparent at first glance. The Abraham narratives include only one that might correspond to this cycle: 15:7–21. In this instance, however, it is an earlier narrative on which 15:7–21 is based that describes an encounter with God similar to those found in the Jacob narratives; in the later form of the narrative, this encounter has been transformed into a promise narrative. Of the Jacob narratives that contain an encounter with God, not one is an original promise narrative.

28:10–22, Jacob's dream at Bethel. One might call this narrative an etiology, that is, a sanctuary foundation narrative, and say that Israel appropriated this sacred site dating from ages past by telling how it was established by the patriarch Israel. The point of such a cult foundation saga would be this: at this spot our father had an encounter with God. This categorization, however, does not do justice to the narrative as a whole. If Genesis 28:10–22 were really just the answer to the question "How did Bethel come to be a sanctuary?" there would be many conceivable answers, and the story would have the character of a piece of information in narrative form. But Genesis 28:10–22 gives the impression of being a genuine narrative, told for its own sake. To be sure it does not involve a tension that is brought to resolution, but in place of the tension we find something analogous: surprise. This surprise speaks so clearly from the narrative in its present form that we have to assume it is an original element. But the element of surprise goes with the framing of the narrative as an encounter on a journey. Jacob's experience of this encounter while traveling determines the entire narrative. This alone can explain verses 10, 11, 16, and 17, especially the way Jacob's cry of alarm is formulated in 16 and 17.

85

But this observation reveals a strand in 28:10–22 that does not form part of the etiology: it belongs to the group of journey reports and is a stopping-place episode expanded into a narrative (it is almost an "adventure" and has been called a "discovery saga"). A major argument for this interpretation, it seems to me, is the observation that there is never any actual theophany. Jacob's alarm ("How awesome is this place!") is not followed by "Fear not!" The sacred site remains awesome and alarming; the god who dwells here does not reveal himself. In the morning Jacob pays cultic homage to the unknown god who dwells here (*'ēl bêt-'ēl*), but this homage seems more an apotropaic propitiation of the god whose domain Jacob has invaded than an act of devotion.

With this original sense, the narrative of the encounter with God in 28:10–22 probably belongs to the earliest stratum of the patriarchal stories. Von Rad states (*Genesis*, Old Testament Library [Philadelphia: Westminster, 1972], p. 285), "The narrator has preserved here a tone of original ancient piety, the effect of whose cogent simplicity is timeless."

There is no need here to discuss the subsequent development of the narrative with the appended oath and the interpolated promise (see above).

32:2–3, Mahanaim. This narrative is precisely parallel in origin to 28:10ff. Its etiological strand differs from that of 28:10ff. in that it does not recount the foundation of a cultic site but merely explains why the site is called Mahanaim. This makes it an onomastic etiology; these always or almost always appear as motifs within narratives. A mere onomastic etiology does not itself constitute a narrative. This account, too, is really a journey episode, as verse 1 shows clearly enough: "Jacob went on his way and there met him . . . ." The episode was once developed into a narrative which is no longer extant. A parallel is found in Joshua 5:13–15, which is also clearly fragmentary. That the original narrative has not been preserved is shown by the discrepancy between *maḥănēh* and *maḥănayim.*

The messengers of God turn up in Genesis 18, 28, and 32. In Joshua 5:13–15, as in Genesis 18, the messenger is addressed by the person to whom he appears. He appears on earth in human form. At one time there was probably a cycle of narratives telling of encounters with such *mal'ākîm*. It is a striking fact that the narrative in 32:2–3 occupies the same position as Joshua 5:13–15, that it appears in the same context. Both serve as introductions to major and perilous undertakings facing those to whom the *mal'āk* appears. Was the angelic encounter at one time associated more closely with undertakings of this nature?

32:23–33, *Peniel*. The encounter at Peniel belongs to the same group of narratives of encounters with God during journeys as Genesis 28:10ff. and 32:2–3. The difference is that here the "adventure" turns into a fight and Jacob experiences his escape from this attack as deliverance; the naming of Peniel at the end (v. 31) is an expression of praise cast in the form of a report.

This is a narrative in the strict sense. Here, too, it begins with a surprise; the encounter turns into an assault, a surprise attack. The tension is heightened in the struggle between Jacob and his opponent, and the resolution is Jacob's escape with the blessing he has won. This strand of the narrative is independent of the etiology. It is clearer here than in 28 that the etiological motif is an added element, which did not shape the narrative.

It is a highly strange and unusual feature that the blessing in this narrative is won in personal combat with a divine being. This contradicts Genesis 27, and in fact everything else that is said about blessings in Genesis. Equally striking and unusual is the observation that this is the only narrative of personal combat in Genesis.

It is impossible to discuss these two peculiarities in detail here. It must suffice to point out that personal combat, a form of combat that plays such an important role in the sagas of other peoples, appears only this once, in the form of a struggle with a divine being. If the prize in this combat is a power transmitted from the vanquished to the victor, this suggests that the narrative was originally mythological and was included in the patriarchal stories with little change.

35:1–7, Bethel. This account is not a narrative in the true sense. It is an account of God's instructions to Jacob (v. 1) and his performance of them. These instructions refer to the earlier appearance of God at Bethel (vv. 1 and 7). The passage serves to bracket a much larger unit in an original way not encountered elsewhere. Genesis 28:10–22 stands between the two narrative complexes 27:1–45 and 29—31; 35:1–7 (if we omit chapter 34) follows the narrative complex 32—33. This bracketing function is emphasized several times in 35:1–7: verse 1, ". . . when you fled from your brother Esau," and verse 7. Can the nature of this bracketing be defined more precisely? The definition of the God to whom Jacob is to build an altar given in verse 1, "the God who appeared to you when . . . ," is repeated with different words in verse 3: "the God who answered me in the day of my distress and has been with me wherever I have gone." This is clearly the language of reporting praise, thanksgiving offered to the God who has delivered the worshiper from past distress. Here, however, the thanksgiving offered by Jacob consists in the building of an altar in the place where God appeared to him. This, then, is the bracketing: following the successful resolution of his mortal conflict with his brother, Jacob offers homage to the God who preserved him through every danger, according to his promises, the God who had appeared to him when he was still in flight.

Here I find the primary strand in 35:1–7. To it was joined the other strand, the commandment to put away the foreign gods, a self-contained episode having nothing directly to do with the other and remaining a separate entity within the pericope. Alt has offered an explanation of this episode in his study "Die Wallfahrt von Bethel nach Sichem" (*Kleine Schriften*, I, pp. 79–88). But we cannot accept the part of his explanation that considers verses 2–4 a unit. Verse 3 refers to verse 1, not to verse 2. Above all, God's command in verse 1 says nothing of renouncing foreign gods, and the fulfillment of this command is reported in verse 7, again without any hint of this renunciation, which is rather a command from Jacob (v. 2) and is carried out as such (v. 4). The journey commanded in verse 1 ("Arise, go up to Bethel") and undertaken by Jacob in verse 3 ("Let us arise and go up to Bethel") has nothing to do with the renunciation; it is rather a pilgrimage (with echoes of the language used in pilgrimage hymns) in fulfillment of an oath.

In other words, 35:1–7 is a report of God's instructions, issued with a liturgical ceremony in view, primarily an act of homage (building an altar) to God for guiding and preserving Jacob from the time of his initial flight to his return. The renunciation of foreign gods associated with this act of homage was a later addition. Both the pilgrimage in fulfillment of an oath and the renunciation are liturgical practices belonging to the period when Israel was settled in Canaan.

SUMMARY: TYPES AND FORMS OF NARRATIVE IN 25—36

The major forms are the same as in 12—25: itineraries, genealogical notices, narratives, plus the promise motif. There are no promise narratives in 25—36.

The narratives themselves, taken as a whole, exhibit an essential difference: the major component of 25—36 is a group of connected narratives that in the nature of their composition fall midway between the brief, self-contained Abraham stories and the Joseph narrative, which constitutes a far larger and more complex unit.

One large complex tells of the rivalry between two brothers (a highly elaborated conflict narrative); its first section, 27:1–45, culminates in the decision of one to slay the other and the latter's flight. The second section reports the return of the refugee, his submission, and the final reconciliation of the two brothers (32—33). Between the two is inserted a necessary but independent interlude: Jacob and Laban (29—31). This is likewise a conflict narrative, albeit very different, culminating in a compact.

Alongside this group of connected narratives that dominates the whole complex, which could be called a single major narrative, there runs a strand of independent minor narratives like those of the Abraham cycle, which have been artfully interwoven with the major narrative.

(a) Before the major narrative come two telescoped birth narratives (25:21–26a), of which verses 21, 24–26a actually constitute a parallel to the narratives of the barren woman in the Abraham cycle. Verses 22–23 are an inquiry and oracle. Then follow the anecdote of the pottage (25:27–34, rivalry) and the P account of Jacob and Esau (26:34–35). The section concludes with 27:46 and 28:1–9, consisting essentially of narrative expansions of genealogical entries.

(b) The major narrative is linked with three narratives of divine encounters, which have been so interwoven as to seem like episodes in the major narrative: 28:10–22; 32:2–3; and 32:23–33. The conclusion of the major narrative is followed in 35:1–7 by a divine commission, analogous to the divine encounters, instructing Jacob to build an altar at Bethel; this passage constitutes a conscious liturgical conclusion to the entire complex.

(c) Interpolated in the midst of the Laban narrative is 29:31–30:24, a totally independent section describing the birth and naming of Jacob's children. As we read this section now, it consists of genealogical entries expanded by an explanation of each name. Closer observation, however, reveals a remarkable work of art. The names of the children, or, more precisely, the explanation of these names, represent an entire drama: the drama of the rivalry between Jacob's two wives. The motif of the "women's conflict," an important motif in the family narrative represented by extended narratives in the Abraham cycle, returns here with an astonishing abundance of individual motifs. The narratives, however, are not developed, but linked together, as it were, in nuce, crystalized in the point of each explanation. It is noteworthy that the narratives present here in nuce detailing the conflict between the women correspond in every way to the narratives of this type in the Abraham cycle. But the conflict between the women is not so prominent as it was; it has retreated a bit into the background. This may be connected with the increased importance of the rivalry between men expressed in the major narrative. But even the narratives of the conflict between the women, reduced to explanations of names, are no longer merely individual stories but have also been put together in narrative sequence, so that these narrative vignettes have a coherent dramatic development from the birth of Leah's first child to the birth of Rachel's last. An entire narrative cycle with this dramatic development can be discerned behind the stylized form of 29:1—30:24.

(d) Following 35:7 there are no true narratives, but rather genealogical entries and lists, in part with narrative expansion (for example, the report of Rachel's death in 35:16–20), itineraries like 35:21 and verse 27, and in 35:22 (Reuben's crime) an abstract of a narrative.

(e) The small units incorporated in the major narrative complexes deserve further study, which must take place in the context of exegesis of the individual passages.

(f) Theologically, the whole narrative cycle of Jacob and Esau is determined by the concept of blessing. The object of the rivalry between the brothers is a blessing. Even the interlude of Jacob and Laban deals with this blessing (the consequences of the blessing in the fertility of Jacob's flock, the effect of the blessing beyond the individual receiving it); the central section of this interlude, which deals with the birth and naming of Jacob's children, is concerned with the blessing of children.

SUMMARY

In previous studies of the types of narrative in Genesis, the general categories of "saga," and more particularly "etiological saga," have had particular importance. When attempting to define these two types more precisely, scholars have been primarily concerned with the relationship between historical reality and the narrative content of the saga or etiological saga. Both analyses have resulted in major progress in explaining the narrative of Genesis. But the definition of sagas and etiological motifs has remained too general and summary, and often too abstract. As a consequence, a greater and greater gulf came to separate the narratives from the reality they reflect.

The study presented here has attempted to progress beyond a general determination of the types of narrative in Genesis. Following the lead of such scholars as Alt, it begins with the promise narratives and shows that the promise motif belongs in large measure not to the period when the patriarchal narratives originated, but to the later period when they were being collected, reshaped, and assembled. But in those cases where the promise motif is rooted in the narratives themselves, it is found in family narrative, defined (following Jolles) as a quite distinct narrative genre in which all the essential action takes place in the realm of the family. A totally different type of narrative appears in Genesis 1–11, where all the narratives share the basic motif of crime and punishment; their locus is not the family but the whole wide world.

Within the family narratives of Genesis 12–50, the three cycles 12–25, 25–36, and 37–50 exhibit in turn strikingly different character. The third of these cycles, the Joseph story, has been omitted because as a major narrative, a kind of novella, it belongs to a later stage. But major differences can be found between the narrative style of the Abraham cycle and that of the Jacob/Esau cycle (only very small fragments of an Isaac cycle have been preserved). The narratives of the Abraham cycle are concerned remarkably often with birth and death; they focus especially on the peril and preservation of the matriarch and her child, so that the vertical structure of the succession of generations dominates the Abraham stories. The Jacob/Esau stories, on the other hand, are determined more by the horizontal structure of the relationship between brothers; many of them are based on the conflict narrative genre. When this motif appears in the Abraham cycle, the conflict is over territory and food; in the Jacob/Esau cycle, it is basically a conflict over property. In addition, conflict between women is an important narrative motif in both cycles; this conflict is over position, honor, and the rights of sons and family. In the Abraham cycle, purely elemental and personal episodes predominate in the narratives; in the Jacob/Esau cycle, the incidents are more differentiated and include institutional elements. Theologically, the Abraham narratives have been shaped secondarily by a strong emphasis on the promise motif; the Jacob/Esau narratives focus on blessing. Sanctuary narratives have been interpolated primarily in the Jacob/Esau cycle; it should also be noted that these did not originate as cultic etiologies but as narratives of divine encounters in the context of journey reports. The Abraham cycle also includes narrative forms that are obviously later, such as descriptions of success and theological narratives.

It must be emphasized in conclusion that this analysis provides only the grossest outline of the nature and arrangement of the Genesis narratives. It must be followed up and developed in detail. Nevertheless, even the types of narrative distinguished here exhibit a stage in the growth of the patriarchal stories that is clearly earlier and distinct from their written redaction. It is a prehistorical stage in which the family is the determinative social form. In this stage we cannot distinguish events, dates, and facts such as constitute the foundation of historical processes, but rather certain fundamental aspects of life in this prehistorical stage, which have been given narrative form: the significance of the succession of generations, the peril and miraculous preservation of mother and child, the conflict between men over territory and food and then over property, the conflict between women over position and honor, divine encounters and discovery of the sacred. We discern a stage prior to the epoch of the extended cult, when relationship to God moves within the realm of the family. But even the comparatively meager stock of patriarchal narratives exhibits so many stratifications and alterations that they reflect already what was probably a highly differentiated history of all the incidents and relationships mentioned.

Beyond this stage, however, the circle of family narrative is surrounded by a larger circle of narratives reflecting the encounter with the distant, alien, and usually sinister world, the narratives of the primal history, which speak of misdeeds, God's punishment, and his mercy.

The Promises to
the Fathers

I
Historical Survey

The promises to the patriarchs could not be the subject of independent study as long as Wellhausen's thesis was generally accepted, that the patriarchal stories as a whole were idealized retrojections from the period of the monarchy. Neither could such a question arise for Gunkel or Gressman, because for them the patriarchal stories were the product of popular fantasy, like fairy tales. The question of the promises is addressed by Staerk (W. Staerk, *Studien zur Religions- und Sprachgeschichte des Alten Testaments, I* [Berlin: Reimer, 1899], pp. 21ff.), who diverges at this point from Gunkel and Gressmann, studying the promises for the first time in their context.

The modern era of study was inaugurated by Galling (K. Galling, *Die Erwählungstraditionen Israels,* BZAW 48 [Giessen: Töpelmann, 1928], §4: "Die Erzväterverheissungen," pp. 37–56), on whose work later scholars built. He takes the position that in the promises "there is reflected the faith of the writers in God's actions in history" (p. 38). According to him, Israel's "election faith" has a double form, being expressed in the exodus traditions and in the patriarchal traditions. Galling describes how this election faith is developed in the four narrative strands (L, J, E, P), here following Staerk. He then discusses how the two election traditions are linked (§5).

It is significant that Galling takes as his starting point the abstract theological concept of "election faith," expressed variously by the various narrators. The approach to the subject is intellectual and abstract, and the subject itself is defined in abstract intellectual terms. Galling examines an ideal that takes varying form in different traditions, failing to see that the texts themselves do not speak in those terms. He does not notice, for instance, that only the latest stratum of the Old Testament (Ps. 105:6–7; Neh. 9:7) looks back on these events as a mark of "election." At the very least, this circumstance shows clearly that election is an interpretative category applied to the promises long after the fact.

When Galling takes as his starting point the election faith of writers during the period of the monarchy (J, L, E, P), it is already assumed that the promises could only have come into being during the literary stage. The question of what function the promises might have had in the patriarchal period is eliminated from the outset.

Galling accordingly considers the promises to the patriarchs only as a whole; what is promised, to whom and in what situation, is irrelevant. His extended discussion of the promises never deals with a specific promise such as the promise of the land or the promise of descendants. At one point he makes the pregnant statement: "The meaning is the same as what we have been calling the patriarchal traditions" (p. 64).

It is also this abstract meaning that, according to Galling, links "the two forms of the election traditions" (p. 63): "What the two traditions have in common is the fundamental attitude of those who live within it: the election faith" (p. 92).

Starting with Alt, Galling's thesis that all the promise texts in

Genesis 12—50 came into being during the written stage of transmission came under attack. It was usually not recognized, however, that the abstract concept of election is a very late secondary interpretative category, inappropriate for describing the phenomena of the promises to the fathers. This abstract and intellectual view of the promises exerted a continuing influence on scholarship.

The work of Alt (A. Alt, "The God of the Fathers," in his *Essays on Old Testament History and Religion* [Oxford: Blackwell, 1966], pp. 1–77; originally published in 1929) represents a new beginning in the study of the promises to the fathers. Alt follows Galling's lead (p. 62), but disputes his conclusions with respect to the promises. The election of Abraham and his descendants goes back to the religion of the gods of the fathers (p. 63). "It can be seen that when the Yahwist and the Elohist go out of their way to link the theme of the divine choice and promise with these gods, their tradition reproduces the historical facts. This is what we would expect from the essential character of these gods as the guide and guardian of their group of worshippers" (pp. 64–65). As soon as the possibility of reproducing historical facts is raised, the real individual promises come under scrutiny, for they reflect the gods' "providential concern for the basic needs of the tribes" (p. 65).

But this immediately raises the question of whether the "content" of the promises can be differentiated. "Moreover, the promises are concerned almost exclusively with two matters, the increase of the patriarchs' posterity, and their possession of the Promised Land. Here again it almost seems as if two separate sets of ideas have been combined, one originating before the entry, and the other in Palestine itself. On the one hand there is the concern of a nomadic tribe for the maintenance and increase of its numbers, on the other the claim of settlers to own their land" (p. 65). This tentative distinction of different promises, suggesting different situations and different periods, has not been sufficiently observed by subsequent scholars. The tendency has been rather to adopt a uniform and more abstract understanding of the promises, following Galling more than Alt.

This thesis proposed by Alt, which followed from his assumption of a special religion of the fathers, traces of which can still be recognized, marks the beginning of study of the promises as events belonging to the patriarchal period.

The effect of Alt's study on the "God of the fathers" was astounding; his thesis was later modified and corrected, but it marked a decisive turning point in the problem of the patriarchs and their religion. It is presupposed in most recent summaries that discuss the period and religion of the patriarchs. But it is significant that after Alt, scholarly interest focused entirely on the problem of the "God of the fathers" as such, as the wealth of literature shows. This circumstance is due to the conviction, adopted uncritically from the nineteenth-century science of religion, that religion is really and essentially concerned with the idea and concept of God; to study a religion is more or less identical with studying the god of that religion. This is a methodology deriving from western thought and governed by medieval theology: all the theological systems of the Middle Ages begin with a chapter *De Deo*.

In the ancient religions themselves, however, the fundamental question is never the idea or concept of God, but the question of the relationship between God (or the gods) and man (cf. C. Westermann, "Das Verhältnis des Jahweglaubens zu den ausserisraelitischen Religionen," in his *Forschung am Alten Testament*, Theologische Bücherei 24 [Munich: Kaiser, 1964], pp. 189–218, especially p. 190). The promises to the fathers have an important bearing on this question, if only because most of the speeches of God in Genesis 12—50 are promises (as noted by J. Blythin, "The Patriarchs and the Promise," *Scottish Journal of Theology* 21 [1968]: 56–73; W. H. Schmidt, *Alttestamentlicher Glaube und seine Umwelt*, Neukirchener Studienbücher 6 [Neukirchen: Neukirchener Verlag,

1968], §3, p. 22). But scholars lost interest in the promises. There are few studies devoted to them, and these few deal for the most part with special facets. There is no truly comprehensive study of the promise texts in Genesis 12—50; the closest thing is J. Hoftijzer's *Die Verheissungen an die drei Erzväter* (Leiden: Brill, 1956).

The effects of Alt's differentiated view of the promises can be seen on the very first page of von Rad's essay "The Promised Land and Yahweh's Land in the Hexateuch," in his *The Problem of the Hexateuch and Other Essays* (Edinburgh: Oliver and Boyd, 1966), pages 79–102 (originally published in 1943). Von Rad lists (pp. 79–80) all the promises in Genesis 12—50, categorized as promises of land, progeny, blessing, and a new relationship with God. This summary delimits the area for future study (even if certain details are altered). Von Rad himself, however, focuses his study entirely on the promise of the land. For him this is the real, determinative promise. "First in importance we must place the oath made to the early patriarchs, i.e. the promise of the land" (p. 79). He asks, "How did he [the Yahwist] come to include the whole mass of patriarchal sagas within the scheme of the promise of land in this way? Alt has given us the answer in his book on the God of the patriarchs: it is because the promise of the land is an original element of the pre-Mosaic cultus of the God of the patriarchs. Here we are in the presence of very oldest tradition. The God of the patriarchs had already promised possession of the land to the ancestors of Israel when they lived in tents on the edge of the settled territory" (p. 83). Here von Rad has not observed the fine distinction made by Alt, who is inclined to assign the promise of progeny to an earlier stratum than the promise of the land. Von Rad then goes on to assess "the order of priority of the various elements within the promise," commenting: "On the face of the matter our survey showed that the promise of land predominated decisively here . . . . The promise of innumerable progeny may have been in some way coordinate with it, but . . . it not unnaturally lost some of its relevance once an account had been given of the birth of the nation in Egypt" (p. 84).

But the absolute priority of the promise of the land in the list of promises is not all that secure; the initial survey reveals a greater number of passages involving the promise of many descendants. The statement that this latter promise lost its relevance may be true for a late stage of tradition, but not for the patriarchal period. What is more important, the question of priority is evaluative; the individual promises should first be examined to determine their function and significance without any evaluation. Von Rad's essay points in this direction; further study had to follow his lead.

Noth (A History of Pentateuchal Traditions [Englewood Cliffs: Prentice-Hall, 1972], pp. 54–58) must be mentioned briefly here because these few pages have been much cited, almost always with concurrence. Noth is not interested in the promises themselves; only the "theme" promise in its significance is important for the growth of the Pentateuch. He takes Alt as his starting point, expressing total agreement but recording Alt's new understanding of the promises (see above) only in vague terms. He says of the cult of the gods of the fathers: "This type of cult, which was absolutely unique, . . . was characterized by a personal relationship of the deity to his worshipers. . . . This religion included above all the divine promise of the inheritance of the land and a numerous posterity who would enjoy this inheritance" (p. 55). Noth considers that "as the descendants of these patriarchs came to settle down on the soil of the arable land . . . the divine promise . . . was considered to have been definitely fulfilled" (p. 55), without asking what it means that afterwards promise and fulfillment became separated through the transition to a different way of life. The promises have for him an essential function in the structuring of the Pentateuch: "It introduced the great historico-theological thread of 'promise

and fulfilment' which binds together the entire work from beginning to end on the basis of the identification of the gods of the
fathers . . . with the God who brought Israel out of Egypt . . ."
(p. 56). This statement in particular has exercised great influence and has been adopted by many scholars. But it has been
overlooked that the arch of tension from promise to fulfillment
in Exodus—Numbers begins with the promise in Exodus 3:7f.
(compare Exodus 6) and concludes in the occupation with the
fulfillment of this promise, which leads up to the exodus.

In Zimmerli's essay "Promise and Fulfillment" (in *Essays on
Old Testament Hermeneutics*, ed. C. Westermann [Richmond:
John Knox, 1963], pp. 89–122), the overall approach is theological; the promises to the patriarchs are dealt with in one section
only (pp. 89–97). Zimmerli continues the course set by Galling
and Alt. Like von Rad, in referring to Alt's work he mentions
only the promise of the land, which he considers the original
form of the promise. "The original content of the promise to the
fathers may have consisted in the pledge of the land" (pp. 91–
92). He states more plainly, however, that this is still just a conjecture. "Very early, however, the pledge of a great posterity was
ranked alongside it. The extensive elaboration of this element,
so powerfully emphasized through the use of the suspense-build-
ing motif of the childless wife in all three patriarchal stories, was
probably due to the combination of patriarchal history with the
Exodus tradition" (p. 92). Zimmerli still does not see that this
suspense motif leads necessarily to the promise of a son, but not
—or at least not necessarily—to the promise of many descendants.
Like von Rad (in his list on pp. 79–80) and most other scholars,
Zimmerli includes both under the heading "promise of descendants." It will be shown, however, that the two were originally
distinct and have different origins.

Having discussed the promise of the land and of many descendants, Zimmerli—like von Rad—goes on to emphasize the
especially important promise text Genesis 12:1–3. "The vitality

101

of the conception of promise may be seen in another way in the introductory passage of the Abraham story formed by the Yahwist. The word of Yahweh to Abraham . . . indeed sounds the note of land and posterity as elements of promise, but it clearly places them in the shadow of the pledge of a blessing (unmistakable in the fivefold use of the root *brk*). . . . This theme of the patriarchal history, newly composed by the Yahwist, can only be understood against the background of the theme of the 'curse' stories in Genesis 3–11" (p. 92). Zimmerli finds here "an expression of a deepening interpretation of the simple land and posterity promises" (pp. 92–93). "The old patriarchal history, which looked forward to fulfillment in the Conquest, is thereby placed in the tension of a much farther-looking expectation of fulfillment. . . . Beyond his account of fulfillment, promise yet unredeemed will remain open" (p. 93).

In his discussion of Genesis 12:1–3 (which is then taken up by H. W. Wolff), Zimmerli deals only with the conception of the Yahwist; like von Rad, Wolff, and most recent exegetes, he considers the promise theme a new contribution on the part of the Yahwist. This assumption does not even admit the question whether the promise may be based on an earlier tradition, going back to the patriarchal period. On this point, Maag espouses the surprising thesis that behind Genesis 12:1–3 there stands an ancient motif from the patriarchal period.

In his two studies ("Der Hirte Israels," *Schweizerische Theologische Umschau* 28 [1958]: 2–28; "Malkût Jhwh," *Supplements to Vetus Testamentum* 7 [1960]: 129–53), whose approach is both religio-historical and sociological, Maag departs from the generally accepted view that Genesis 12:1–3 is an original creation of the Yahwist. He uses this text as the most important piece of evidence for his thesis that in the patriarchal narratives we can still recognize nomadic transmigration. "In Genesis, the deity's function as leader and guide on every step of the way is evident. Gen. 12:1 . . . reflects an event that occurs not infrequently . . . in the nomadic way of life: the separation of one part of a tribe from the whole to live independently when pasturage grows insufficient, and . . . transmigration to new pasturage" ("Hirte," p. 10; elaborated in "Malkût," p. 138).

Now, of course, Genesis 12:1–3 does not contain any promise of land. On this point Maag says, ". . . thus both [transmigration traditions] contain the imperative to transmigrate. Religio-historically, however, it would be a totally unique and incomprehensible phenomenon for this imperative to occur in one tradition without a promise. Without a promise it could never be accepted" ("Malkût," pp. 140–41, n. 2). But Maag (rejecting Hoftijzer's thesis) distinguishes the promise which is necessary for transmigration from the promise of *possession* of land in the Genesis texts "This . . . agrees *to a certain extent* with the conclusions reached by the history of religions: the notion of *possession* of land and of *national* existence are not among the primary desiderata of nomadic tribes. Precisely because of this secondary character of the two elements (in their present form), they have nothing to say about the original character of the patriarchal religion" ("Malkût," p. 141, n. 2). Thus Maag disputes the position that sees Genesis 12:1–3 as an original creation of the Yahwist; he sees it as being based on an extremely early tradition. This departure leads him to distinguish the promise of *possession* of the land, which cannot derive from a purely nomadic way of life, from a promise associated with transmigration, associated with the command to depart: the promise of new territory or pasturage. The problem with this thesis is that such a promise is only vaguely hinted at in Genesis 12:1, in the words "to the land that I will show you." Furthermore, no narratives mentioning transmigration appear in Genesis 12—50. What is important, however, is Maag's observation that the promises must involve those that correspond to the "primary desiderata" of nomadic groups (as already suggested by Alt).

In addition, Maag finds a further, independent promise in the statement "I will be with you" (for example, Gen. 28:15), a promise of presence and help that likewise belongs to the situation of transmigration. This formula has been studied by H. D. Preuss and D. Vetter (see below).

In Hoftijzer's work (*Die Verheissungen an die drei Erzväter* [Leiden: Brill, 1956]) the pendulum moves in the opposite direction. While Maag finds a very ancient nucleus in the promises that had previously been considered an original creation of the Yahwist (12:1–3), Hoftijzer locates the entire complex of the promises in the late period around the time of the exile.

At the start, Hoftijzer surveys the results of previous scholarship (pp. 1–5). In opposition to the scholars following Alt, he objects, "It seems to me incorrect to ask this question (about earlier stages) before . . . examining the significance of the forms of the tradition that have been preserved . . . in their present context" (p. 5). In chapter 1 he brings together "the Genesis material," which he divides into two groups: the El Shaddai group (all P passages) and the Genesis 15 groups (everything else). Examination of the passages in their context (pp. 14ff.) reveals that each group has a central text (Genesis 15 and 17) in which the promise is an integral part of the narrative, while elsewhere the promises are literarily or traditio-historically secondary in their context. In chapters 2–4, Hoftijzer examines the material outside Genesis and then in chapter 5 comes to the problem of earlier stages. Here he carries on his debate with Alt, whose thesis he disputes. "In the promise traditions themselves, as they have come down to us, we can find no reason to conclude that there was an earlier stage" (p. 97). "A promise tradition did not come into existence until there was a connection . . . between the patriarchal period and the exodus period" (p. 98). ". . . then the tradition of the promises to the three patriarchs is a late tradition . . . the forms known to us [must] all be dated in a period when the existence of the nation was imperiled or when the nation was in exile, in other words, quite late" (p. 99).

The first thing that must be said of Hoftijzer's work is positive: his methodological starting point, the insistence that *all* the promise texts must be examined and that they must be examined in their present context, must be acknowledged. Such an attempt had been made by Staerk and likewise by Galling, but no inclusive study was made subsequently. At the same time, it must be said that Hoftijzer's study is quite summary. As a consequence, uncritically following the lead of earlier scholars, he reduced the many promises to the promise of the land and descendants, mentioning other promises only on rare occasions. With full recognition of Hoftijzer's methodological requirement, the promise texts still must be studied more thoroughly and from various perspectives. It follows from his methodological requirement, however, that from now on studies that fail to take account of the whole body of texts will be of dubious worth.

Hoftijzer is also right in insisting that the context of each promise must be examined. This insistence led him to the important observation that promises that are an integral part of a narrative must be distinguished from those that have been appended or interpolated secondarily. This established a new and important criterion for the traditio-historical study of the promises, a criterion adopted and extended in the work of Westermann. Hoftijzer found in each group a single narrative in which the promise was an original component of the narrative (Genesis 15 and 17). Since he was considering only the promise of the land and the promise of many descendants, he failed to see that in chapter 18 we have a narrative of which a promise is a necessary part, the promise of a son. Hoftijzer did not recognize this as an independent promise with its own significance. Subsequent observation that the promise of a son has clear parallels in the Ugaritic texts that are roughly contemporary with the patriarchal period (see below) casts severe doubt on Hoftijzer's entire hypothesis. But his methodological insights have advanced scholarship significantly. (Reviews: M. Noth, *Vetus Testamentum* 7 [1957]: 430–33; J. Hempel, *Bibliotheca Orientalis* 15 [1958]: 44–45; R. de Vaux, *Revue Biblique* 65 [1958]: 132–33; A. S. Herbert, *Journal of Semitic Studies* 2 [1957]: 399–400.)

Hoftijzer's thesis was taken up once more by J. Van Seters

("Confessional Reformulation in the Exilic Period," *Vetus Testamentum* 22 [1972]: 448–59). He takes as his starting point the observation that Jeremiah and Ezekiel speak only of the "fathers" after the exodus; the same would hold for the many Deuteronomy passages mentioning the promise of the land if the appending of the names of the patriarchs to the term "fathers" were a later addition. Everywhere else the patriarchs are mentioned in early texts we are dealing with late additions. A late (exilic) period is also suggested by Exodus 15:7. Van Seters concludes: "It seems to me that the confession of Yahweh as the God of the patriarchs and the association of the promises to the fathers with the patriarchs is a specific development of Israel's sacred traditions during the exilic period and directly related to the needs of that period. . . . The 'god of the fathers' religion and the promises of land and numerous progeny which are integrally related to it, are not the remnant of an early presettlement religion of landless nomads, but the basic components of an exilic religion of homeless exiles" (p. 459).

This interesting and daring hypothesis founders on the fact that the promises are firmly established in the patriarchal narratives themselves. It would have to be claimed that these narratives themselves are exilic. Above all, this hypothesis cannot hold true for the promise of a son.

Westermann (see above, pp. 2–30), following a brief historical survey, discusses the "distribution of the different promises" (pp. 10–30) and inquires into the criteria that could be used to define them more precisely in a traditio-historical sense. He observes initially, "The promise of a son is not identical with the promise of descendants (that is, the promise of many descendants), but represents an independent type" (p. 11). He then adopts Hoftijzer's criterion, that we must ask where a promise is an integral part of a narrative, and finds this holds true in Genesis 18. "The promise forms a necessary part of this narrative, which is based on the problem of childlessness, from the very outset, and is clearly an original element of this narrative" (p. 12).

This narrative yields a further criterion: in an original promise narrative, a single promise is given; the combination of several or many promises points to a secondary stage. The various combinations must be studied in their own right, as well as the promises found in isolation. A third criterion can likewise be derived from the promise of a son: whether the promise and its fulfillment are closely juxtaposed or the fulfillment is set far off from the promise. We can conclude that we are dealing with an early narrative when the fulfillment represents the resolution of a tension arising from an initial situation (in this case the problem of childlessness) addressed by the promise. A fulfillment that does not come until centuries after the promise cannot have been part of the same narrative. It turns out that Genesis 18 is a different sort of narrative than Genesis 15:1–6 and 15:7–21, because only in 18 is a tension brought to resolution. "It turns out, therefore, that only a very small portion of the narratives in Genesis 12—50 were conceived originally as promise narratives. Most of the narratives in which we find promises were transformed secondarily into promise narratives, or else the promises stand outside the ancient narratives as expansions, interpolations, interludes . . ." (p. 28).

Wolff's essay "The Kerygma of the Yahwist" (in *The Vitality of Old Testament Traditions* [Richmond, Va.: John Knox Press, 1975], pp. 41–66; originally published in German in 1964) places all its emphasis on what the Yahwist intended to say in Genesis 12:1–3 to his own age. Following von Rad and Zimmerli, he defines Genesis 12:1–3 as a link between the primal history and the history of the patriarchs (pp. 53–55), and emphasizes in this connection ". . . that the first message of the Yahwist may be seen in 12:3b" (p. 55), which then refers directly to this historical period of Israel. "How are they to find blessing *in Israel*? By Israel's intercession with Yahweh on the example of Abraham;

by readiness for peaceful agreement on the pattern of Isaac; by economic aid on the model of Jacob" (p. 59). But in spite of Wolff's emphasis on the present significance of the promise in Genesis 12:1–3, he also inquires into preceding traditions. For him, too, Genesis 12:1–3 is an original creation of the Yahwist; the last statement in particular had never been made before (p. 63). These words, then, could never have been heard by Abraham. But Wolff does inquire into the earlier history of the preceding sentences. Like von Rad, he expresses surprise that the promise of the land, which was certainly familiar to the Yahwist, recedes totally into the background in 12:1–3 (p. 49). It is heard only as a faint echo in 12:1b: "The theme is reduced by the Yahwist almost to a footnote" (p. 49). Wolff does not mention the possibility that the command to depart might contain an ancient tradition from the patriarchal period (see the discussion of Maag above). With the promise of many descendants, however, "The Yahwist thus reaches back to perhaps the oldest, even pre-Palestinian, layer of the patriarchal tradition" (p. 49).

In this connection, Wolff makes a decided advance in the distinction of the individual promises. "Even the principal catchword of our key passage, the word 'blessing' . . . is understandable only from this ancient element of promise . . . having its origin in the promise of a son and descendants respectively; . . . Never is land in earnest of the 'blessing'; land, rather, is simply something Yahweh had unconditionally promised, on his 'oath' . . ." (pp. 49–50). Here Wolff recognizes the special nature of the promise of a blessing (which receives little if any recognition in the preceding studies) and its close relationship with the promise of increase. At the same time, however, Wolff shows how the ancient concept of blessing is changed. "If, in the family structure of the ancients, blessing was understood as an immediately effective and powerful word (see Gen. 24:34–36), then here . . . it is *promised* to future ages. 'Blessing' becomes the linchpin word (*Deutewort*) in the great history of Israel from Abraham's setting out to David's empire" (p. 50). Westermann makes a similar point (*Blessing: In the Bible and the Life of the Church* [Philadelphia: Fortress, 1978], pp. 49–53). "The word of curse or blessing, formed in the cult and spoken by man, becomes the word of promise, spoken by God: 'I will bless!' . . ." (Wolff, "Kerygma," p. 52). Here an important event in the history of the promise has been recognized.

Seebass (*Der Erzvater Israel und die Einführung der Jahwereligion in Kanaan, BZAW* 28 [Berlin: Töpelmann, 1966]) studies the Israel traditions in Genesis, at many points discussing the promise texts. For the history of the study of these texts, the most important point is that Seebass's work exhibits the continued effort to understand the unique features of the individual promises and see the tradition history of each more clearly. In §1 (on Deut. 26:5ff.) he shows the connection between the credal statement that the few in Egypt became a great nation and the promise of increase. Among the texts embodying the promise of the land, he notes the uniqueness of Genesis 28:13 (". . . here it is limited entirely to Bethel and its vicinity" [p. 23]) and concludes that the promise of the land as such originally referred only to the sanctuary of Bethel and its environs. The passage Genesis 28:13 is therefore the origin of the general promise of the land, a conclusion that eliminates this promise from the Abraham-Isaac sagas. Whether such a conclusion can be reached so easily may remain an open question here; for many reasons I do not consider it justified. In similar fashion, Clements (*Abraham and David*, Studies in Biblical Theology, 2d ser., 5 [Naperville: Allenson, 1967], p. 33) finds in chapter 15 the permission of the deity of Mamre (El Shaddai?) for a Hebrew clan led by Abraham to settle in the vicinity of Mamre/Hebron. For historical purposes, it is important to note that the inquiry is dealing with the origin and tradition of the individual promises and their relationship to the individual cycles of the patriarchal history. Thus Seebass says of the promise of descendants that it is a common element. In contrast to Hoftijzer, he considers it an ancient tradition; it points "to very early periods in the prehistory of

Israel." Of course, when Seebass looks for local associations of the various promises with specific sanctuaries, this is out of the question for the early stages of the tradition. The question whether the promises are integral parts of narratives and how individual promises are related to complexes of promises does not concern him.

Herrmann (*Die prophetischen Heilserwartungen im Alten Testament*, BWANT 85 [Stuttgart: Kohlhammer, 1965], "Die Kulturlandverheissung," pp. 64–78) identifies the promise to the fathers with the promise of the settled land; on page 77 he speaks of "expectation of salvation in the form of the promise of the settled land," which he finds in Genesis 12:1–3. He does not mention the actual promises of the land or the many other promises.

Lohfink (*Die Landesverheissung als Eid*, Stuttgarter Bibelstudien 28 [Stuttgart: Katholisches Bibelwerk, 1967]) in his study of Genesis 15 deals intensively with the promises as a whole; this study is especially interesting and valuable for the subsequent course of this investigation. "The present study asks what is the earliest text attesting to the tradition of a covenant with the fathers" (p. 7), and gives the answer: ". . . the earliest witness to the tradition of a covenant with the fathers: Genesis 15" (p. 7). Lohfink takes as his starting point the observation (already made by Wolff) that in both the Yahwist and the Elohist only the promise of the land is termed an oath on the part of Yahweh to the fathers. He devotes particular attention to this promise. First Lohfink surveys the passages outside of Genesis: "They all point directly or indirectly back to Genesis 15, which thus finally is shown to be the earliest accessible text bearing on Yahweh's oath promising the land to Abraham" (p. 23). Lohfink takes Genesis 15 to be an "artificial narrative" (p. 33). "The emphasis of the text is not on the actions described but on the content of what Yahweh says" (p. 34). Later he terms Genesis 15 more precisely an "interpretative secondary collection of oracles" (p. 82). An artificial narrative can comprehend various types of material. "In fact, we find in other Abraham texts of Genesis an independent narrative embodying the promise of a son in Genesis 18:1–16 and an independent composite tradition embodying the promise of the land in Genesis 12:7" (p. 35). The unity of the text is confirmed by these structural correspondences between the two halves. As an artificial narrative, the text of Genesis 15 is a unit, with secondary additions in 15:3 and 15:13–16 (p. 40). We see ". . . that in this text earlier Abraham traditions have emerged into the light of new interpretative categories" (p. 51). These earlier traditions—the promise of a son, the promise of descendants, and the promise of the land—point back to what were originally independent narratives (according to C. Westermann); we may also assume that the promise of the land had an earlier form (p. 52). The interpretative elements are extremely varied: ". . . in the . . . language of the interpretative material we find indirect references to ancient seers and prophets, to oracles of success addressed to a warrior king, to the classical exodus and conquest theology of Israel, to the sacrificial system . . ." (p. 64; here much has been borrowed from O. Kaiser).

In chapter 9 Lohfink asks, "What did Abraham experience?" Here he has left the plane of the artificial narrative, which comprised the whole of chapter 15, and is discussing only the earlier form that can be traced behind Genesis 15:7–21. This was "the narrative of an incubation," a parallel to Genesis 28. But when Lohfink in this chapter looks on 15:7–21 totally in isolation and completely ignores 15:1–6 in discussing the "historical problem," it means that he considers the earlier form of Genesis 15:7–21 to be a separate narrative, totally independent of 15:1–6 (similarly p. 51). This approach undermines his claim that chapter 15 is a single unit (p. 40). If Genesis 15 was not composed by the Yahwist "but was rather available to him already in fixed form" (p. 82), it is hardly possible to say that it "is the product of a single act of literary (or preliterary) creation . . ." (p. 40). Lohfink's study in fact suggests that the chief stress should be placed on the individual narratives to which the present text of Genesis 15 points.

In this case, however, the hypothesis Lohfink takes as his starting point is not so secure. This weakness also appears in chapter 10, "Covenant or Oath?" We can certainly agree with Lohfink (following E. Kutsch) that in Genesis 15:18 krt bryt does not mean "make a covenant," but rather "give assurance under oath," "swear an oath." But what is the traditio-historical significance of this observation for the promise of the land? Lohfink correctly states, "krt berît in v. 18 [is] a statement concerning a unilateral oath sworn by God before Abraham . . ., through which God gave his servant assurance with respect to the promise of the land, which had already been made" (p. 108; my emphasis). And even more pregnantly, "In Genesis 15, then, it is not simply God's promise of the land to Abraham that is narrated, but the oath confirming this promise" (p. 108). The only possible conclusion is that this argument presupposes a form of the promise that did not involve an oath, but was simply a promise. And when Lohfink adds, "The promises of the land to Isaac and to Jacob are not associated in the early narratives with an oath sworn by God" (p. 108), it is obvious that this must be the earlier form that is also presupposed in Genesis 15:7ff. (as assumed also, for example, by Seebass; see above). It is then indeed possible to maintain that Genesis 15 is the earliest text bearing on the oath associated with the promise of the land (p. 7), but not that Genesis 15 is the earliest text bearing on the promise of the land. A new question is also raised, that of the relationship between the texts containing the simple promise of the land and the texts that associate the promise with an oath.

However one may feel about the conclusions Lohfink reaches in his study, it represents a major contribution to the problem of the promises, especially in the realm of methodology.

I. Blythin ("The Patriarchs and the Promise," *Scottish Jour-*

nal of Theology 21 [1968]: 56–73) takes as his starting point the question: "To what extent and in what form can the idea of the promise of the land and descendants be traced back to the patriarchal period?" This question arises from the status of scholarship, whose history he outlines briefly. Once again we must reckon with the possible historicity of the patriarchs and their religion; therefore it is necessary to inquire into the elements of this religion, and above all one of the most important components of Genesis 12–50, the promises. The crucial question is whether this patriarchal religion *necessarily* included the promises of the land and of descendants. Blythin, in agreement with many scholars, considers the essential promises to be the promise of land and of descendants, which he can also call the "twofold promise."

Another question is that of the relationship between the exodus tradition and the patriarchal traditions. In Genesis 15, the ritual of the covenant is undoubtedly early, but it appears "that the structure of the Sinai covenant account was a typus of the patriarchal covenant tradition rather than vice versa." The question remains whether the promise was an original component of the pericope; this applies in any case to the data concerning the extent of the promised land. Blythin notes that in the three Exodus passages where the "God of the fathers" is mentioned, there is no direct reference to any promises, and that in the patriarchal stories themselves (Genesis 12–36) the "God of the fathers" is linked with promises only in three passages (Gen. 26:24; 28:13; 32:10). The exaggerated similes ("like the sand of the sea") in the promise of increase are not really appropriate to the milieu of the patriarchal period; in the case of the promise of the land, also, this is dubious on sociological grounds. It is also noteworthy that the earliest formulation of the creed in Deuteronomy 26 says nothing of any promise (probably without the later formulation in Deuteronomy 6).

What is crucial for Blythin is the relationship between promise and blessing. He adopts Westermann's explanation of Genesis 12:1-3, namely that the promise of blessing represents an original contribution by the Yahwist, who transformed the ahistorical blessing into a historical promise. The blessing in its original form (as in Genesis 27) undoubtedly belongs to the patriarchal period; in the case of the promises, considerable evidence points to later composition.

In conclusion, we shall mention a few studies dealing with non-Israelite parallels to the patriarchal promises. Up to now such parallels have played no role in scholarship on the problem of the promises. Among the parallels cited by Alt in his discussion of the God of the fathers and subsequent additional parallels cited by later scholars, there was no occurrence of the promise motif.

Eissfeldt ("Der kanaanäische El as Geber der den israelitischen Erzvätern geltenden Nachkommenschaft- und Landbesitzverheissungen," *Studia Orientalia in memoriam C. Brockelmann* [= *Wissenschaftliche Zeitschrift der Martin-Luther-Universität Halle-Wittenberg* 12 (1968), pp. 45–53]; reprinted in his *Kleine Schriften*, V [Tübingen: Mohr, 1973], pp. 50–62), following a study published by Brockelmann in 1922, proposes the thesis ". . . that it was originally the Canaanite El deities that gave the promises of descendants and land to the Israelite patriarchs" (*Kleine Schriften*, V, p. 52). This assertion is surprising in view of the contrary statement of Alt: "But it is noticeable that the names of the gods of the Fathers regularly appear whenever there is any promise made to the patriarchs" ("God of the Fathers," p. 64). It becomes understandable, however, when one follows Eissfeldt through all the passages (pp. 53–59), where he cites as evidence of this thesis not only the texts that mention El (very few outside of P), but also those in which it can be assumed that the incident takes place at a Canaanite sanctuary, "so that it becomes reasonable to assume that Yahweh has replaced El in 12:7" (p. 53). In this fashion it turns out that the promises to the patriarchs were almost all made by the Canaanite El.

This much can be said for Eissfeldt's thesis: the names such as Bethel and Penuel in early narratives suggest that the divine name El had significance in the patriarchal narratives. That this significance extends specifically to the promises cannot be claimed, because, as Eissfeldt constantly shows, divine names are all too easily interchangeable in the promises.

Eissfeldt makes no inquiry into the character of the texts to which the promises belong. He does not distinguish promises that are components of a narrative and promises that are additions or interpolations. Neither does he inquire into the difference between promises that are fulfilled in the patriarchal period itself and those that are fulfilled in the nation of Israel; he appears a priori to assume the latter for all the promises. Eissfeldt in fact is concerned with only a single question: the one who makes the promises. The promises themselves are as homogeneous for him as they were for Galling. That the individual promises might have independent prehistories does not interest him. This is especially clear in one particular case. It is reasonable to suppose that, if it is El who gives the promises, something similar should appear in the Ugaritic texts. Because for Eissfeldt the promises are *eo ipso* promises of land and descendants, he fails to notice that in fact the promise of a son (which he deliberately excludes, p. 55) has clear parallels in the Ugaritic texts.

These parallels have been pointed out by several scholars, including K. Koch ("Die Sohnesverheissung an den ugaritischen Danel," *Zeitschrift für Assyriologie*, NF 24 [1967]: 211–21). "The two Ugaritic royal epics . . . begin . . . with a lament by the childless hero. In each case the resolution of the distress is shown by a vision that issues in the promise of a son" (p. 211). In the discussion that follows, Koch discusses in detail the "twelve tasks of the (royal) son" (pp. 213–17). He concludes: "All this suggests that we have found here a figure belonging to an earlier religious stage, brought at one time to Ugarit as a nomadic clan religion by a ruling class just settling down. The similarities to the much discussed 'God of the fathers' of the Old Testament patriarchal sagas, who is likewise the tutelary deity of the clan . . . is immediately obvious" (p. 218).

Koch therefore sees ". . . important points of comparison . . . for the theme of the promises to the patriarchs . . ." (p. 221).

This reference by Koch (pointed out earlier, for example, by H. Cazelles, "Patriarches," *Dictionnaire de la Bible*, Supplements 7 [1966], p. 144) to a Ugaritic parallel to the promise of a son appears very important to me. If Koch had examined the text of the promise in more detail in the passages he mentions, it would have been clear at once that the parallel is not limited to the isolated motif of the promise of a son but extends to the sequence of motifs mentioned in the first sentence of his article (see above): childlessness, lament of the childless man, promise of a son, birth of the son, the same sequence that appears in the Abraham cycle Genesis 12–25. This shows that the promise of a son had as its original context a narrative moving from childlessness through the promise to the birth of the child, thus demonstrating the independent significance of the promise of a son, apart from the promise of increase. Koch's lead should be pursued.

Cazelles ("Patriarches," pp. 81–156, especially 144–45) seeks to show by means of ancient Near Eastern parallels to the promises that (contrary to Hoftijzer in particular) in the patriarchal period there had long been promises given by gods to men. In the inscription on the Gudea Cylinder, Ningirsu or Enlil promises Gudea success and a long life; Enlil promises Urnammu a universal reign; we find promises of fertility, extensive expansion of the realm, a glorious name, victories, and conquests. Cazelles also mentions the promises of a son in the Ugaritic texts.

While the Ugaritic promises can be seen as a true parallel to the promise of a son in the patriarchal stories (see above), the oracle of favor addressed to the king is really another matter with other linguistic forms; it cannot be viewed as a parallel in the strict sense to the promises to the patriarchs, which belong to a different cultural *niveau*. It would nevertheless be worthwhile, following Cazelles's lead, to inquire more closely into the relationship between the promises to the king and the promises to the patriarchs.

SUMMARY

The course of scholarship can be easily outlined. With Alt, the problem of the promises to the patriarchs becomes a question involving the patriarchal period itself. For von Rad, Noth, Zimmerli, and Wolff, the emphasis is on the literary phase of the problem, the meaning of the promises for the Yahwist or for the growth of the Pentateuch, although, following Alt, the origin of the promises in the patriarchal period is recognized. We can also recognize a tendency to move beyond undifferentiated treatment of the promises (as in Galling) to a more precise definition of the individual promises. Initially a predominant importance is ascribed to one of the promises: for von Rad and Zimmerli, it is the promise of the land; for Wolff, the promise of blessing.

Next there is revealed an uncertainty: at about the same time the promises are assigned to a very late period (around the exile: Hoftijzer, followed by Van Seters) and to a very early period (Gen. 12:1 belongs to the patriarchal period: Maag). Such discrepancies almost always indicate a methodological dilemma. Alt's thesis of a possible very early origin of the promises had been recognized, but its methodological implications had not yet been explored. At this point the work of Hoftijzer marks a new beginning. He insists on the examination of all the promise texts, each in the context where it now stands, and thus hits upon the distinction between promises as integral components of narrative and independent promise texts. This lead is followed by Westermann, who inquires into the character of the promise narratives, distinguishes various types of promise narrative, and adds the criterion that in the promise narrative proper only a single promise is made. These leads are followed up and extended by Lohfink.

During this period, the unique features of the individual promises and their separate histories are illuminated to a degree. Previously only the promise of the land and the promise of descendants had been considered relevant (as still by Alt), with priority usually given to the promise of the land (e.g., von Rad, Zimmerli). Now von Rad distinguishes four promises: land, descendants, blessing, and a new relationship with God. Wolff shows the unique nature of the promise of blessing and its close relationship to the promise of descendants. Maag distinguishes the promise of land possession from the promise of new pasturage or territory (transmigration). Westermann demonstrates the separate significance of the promise of a son alongside the promise of descendants. Seebass strives to view the individual promises in the context of their separate traditions, distinguishing the general promise of the land from a promise referring only to the environs of Bethel, and inquiring into the relationship of the promises to the individual cycles of the patriarchal history. Lohfink takes as his starting point the observation that only the promise of the land is called an oath sworn to the fathers by Yahweh (as already noted by Wolff), pursues the nature of the promise narrative, and adopts Westermann's criterion that a promise narrative originally contains only a single promise, as well as the independent significance of the promise of a son.

It will probably be of far-reaching significance that a parallel has been found in the Ugaritic texts to the promise of a son (Koch), in the same sequence of motifs that appears in the Abraham narratives.

It is now our task to examine the individual promises on the basis of all the promise texts in the Old Testament, inquiring into their traditions and, whenever possible, their origins.

II

The Promises in General

THE MOTIF OF THE PROMISES IN THE OLD TESTAMENT

It is a peculiarity of the patriarchal history that a series of texts recur within it. They are so similar that this similarity must be considered in exegesis. This peculiarity is most striking in the case of the motif of the promises made to the fathers. It is the most frequent motif in Genesis 12—50 and is therefore of particular importance for an understanding of the patriarchal stories. This motif has therefore for some time attracted the special attention of scholars (see the historical survey above). It is generally agreed that the texts containing the promises cannot be interpreted solely on the basis of their present contexts; they have an extended context also in the group of identical or similar promises in Genesis 12—50 and also beyond Genesis. Thus to the literary context there are added form-critical and traditio-historical contexts. Also, these promises to the fathers are not limited to Genesis 12—50; they are frequently alluded to—most frequently in Deuteronomy, but reference to the promises extends to Nehemiah and the New Testament.[1] Thus the promise motif could be isolated; it exhibits an independent life that suggests special examination. Many studies also begin with the later history, for example, that of van Seters, who starts with the passages in Ezekiel and Jeremiah.

Since Alt, it has been assumed that the promises belong to the earliest stratum of the patriarchal narratives; at the same time, the motif appears in Nehemiah. We must therefore consider a history of the tradition of this motif that might extend from the middle of the second millennium to the third or fourth century.

---

1. On the later history of the promises, see especially the works of Hoftijzer and Van Seters, as well as P. A. H. de Boer, *Gods Beloften over Land en Volk in het OT* (Delft: Gaade, 1955), as well as the work by Lohfink.

Interest in the motif was still alive in this late period. It is clear that this interest of the later period concentrated exclusively on the fulfillment of the promises. This is most obvious in the extraordinary number of references to the promise of the land in Deuteronomy, which is easily explained on the basis of its setting as a discourse by Moses before entrance into the land. Not rarely these passages speak of Abraham, Isaac, and Jacob as recipients of the promise, or call the promise an oath (as in Gen. 15:7ff.) sworn by God to these patriarchs. It is nevertheless not certain that all the passages in Deuteronomy and later books refer to the patriarchs of Genesis 12—50. The text may also refer to the promise given to the generation of the exodus;[2] this is probable in the case of Ezekiel 20:42, which looks back from a great distance to the promises to the fathers. In the late history of the motif, the emphasis is so totally on fulfillment that it became irrelevant whether the promise was made to Abraham or to Moses.

THE PROMISES GIVEN DIRECTLY

The promises belong in the context of all the promises or words of salvation and favor in the Old Testament, in that they all promise or announce to someone something beneficial from God.[3] But they differ from all other groups of words of favor in the Old Testament in that they are not spoken through a mediator of any sort or through cultic mediation, but directly to the patriarchs. This difference is of immense significance, but, as far as I know, it has been almost totally ignored in previous scholarship. In the first place, this observation makes it possible to study the promises to the patriarchs independently, since it applies uniquely to them. In addition, however, this unique feature is

2. Van Seters makes this assumption for all the Deuteronomy passages. On the relationship between the two, see Herrmann (discussed on p. 110 above), especially pages 65ff.
3. S. Herrmann, *Die prophetischen Heilserwartungen im Alten Testament,* BWANT 5 (Stuttgart: Kohlhammer, 1965); C. Westermann, "The Way of the Promise through the Old Testament," in *The Old Testament and Christian Faith,* ed. B. W. Anderson (New York: Harper, 1963), pages 200–24.

an indication that the promises may in fact go back to the patriarchal period, for it is a characteristic feature of the patriarchal
religion that it knows nothing of any mediators, cultic or other-
wise. When cultic acts occur in the patriarchal narratives, it is
the patriarchs themselves who perform them. Other divine discourses, too, such as instructions or commands, are addressed
directly to the patriarchs.[4] This is such a clear criterion for the
relationship between man and God in the patriarchal period that
in it the promises must have preserved at least a reminiscence of
the patriarchal period. This unique feature is highlighted by the
fact that immediately after the patriarchal history, at the beginning of the Book of Exodus, a promise is given through a mediator to the group in Egypt. In both cases the promise is linked
with a command to depart; in Exodus 3, it is addressed through
Moses to those enslaved in Egypt, while in Genesis 12:1ff. it is
given directly. "Now Yahweh said to Abram, 'Go from your
country. . . .'" Even if Genesis 12:1–3 is a composition of the
Yahwist, this distinction must have been alive during the period
of written composition, because in all the promise texts of Genesis 12—50 the promise is spoken directly, without a mediator.

It may be objected that in some places the promises are given
through a mal'ak yhwh or an "angel from heaven." This objection is beside the point, however, because we never find an angel
giving a promise in any of the other groups of words of favor.
The angel is God's representative, not a mediator. The words of
divine favor outside of Genesis 12—50 are transmitted through
someone having the office of a mediator or through cultic
mediation.

Even though this observation suffices to justify separate treatment of the promises to the patriarchs, it does not eliminate the
possibility of points of contact with words of divine favor of
later periods. If the promises had such a long lifetime, they
could have become associated with other types and forms of

4. See pages 182ff.

promise. We must also reckon with the possibility that even in Genesis 12—50 individual promises may have been cloaked in the form of later words of favor. This is the case when a promise to Abraham in 15:1 is introduced by the prophetic word-event formula, when the promise to Abraham in 15:1–6 recalls the form of the later salvation oracle, and when in P a part of the "covenant formula" becomes a promise.[5] This shows that even within Genesis 12—50 the promises cannot all without distinction derive from the patriarchal period, nor can they all without distinction be considered compositions of various writers—the Yahwist, the Elohist, and the author of P. In each case we must rather locate the particular instance on the path of tradition, which can extend from the patriarchal period to the late period of Israel's history.

THE RELATIONSHIP OF THE PROMISES
TO THE NARRATIVES

During the first phase of study of the promises, their great importance for the patriarchal history was emphasized without further inquiry into the relationship between the promises and the patriarchal narratives. For Noth, this is the real theme of Genesis 12—50, which he calls "promise to the patriarchs." Zimmerli says of this promise, "This element of older tradition proved able not only to establish and maintain itself, but also to become dominant in the entire breadth of the patriarchal narratives" (p. 71); "the word about the promise of Yahweh to the fathers seeps into almost all the patriarchal narratives like a liquid dye, giving them the quite specific coloration which distinguishes them even in a superficial reading" (p. 95).[6]

Beginning with Hoftijzer, the question is raised: in what way

5. This appears clearly in P's promise of future greatness to Abraham, where we find the same pair of words ("nations"/"kings") as in Deutero-Isaiah's words of salvation (for example, Isa. 41:2; 45:1); see Hoftijzer, *Die Verheissungen an die drei Erzväter* (Leiden: Brill, 1956), pages 9f.
6. Von Rad says much the same in many passages.

are the promises associated with the patriarchal narratives? And especially, do they belong to the patriarchal narratives themselves as a necessary component? This question finds a surprising answer: there are very few patriarchal narratives in which the promises are integral parts of the narrative. Hoftijzer singled out Genesis 15 and 17. Westermann went on to show that Genesis 15 and 17 are narratives especially constructed for the promises (a view adopted by Lohfink, who calls them "artificial narratives"), whereas chapters 16 and 18 are true promise narratives. The promise of a son, which is the subject matter of 16 and 18, had not been viewed as a separate and distinct promise by Hoftijzer (and earlier scholars). Chapters 16 and 18 belong to the group of family narratives, the most important group among the patriarchal narratives.[7]

In all other cases (with the possible exception of Genesis 28), the promises are not an original component of the narratives but were added to or associated with the narratives in many different ways. We may distinguish the following groups:

(a) The promise constitutes an independent scene. Such a scene occurs in Genesis 13:14–17. It is linked to the preceding narrative by its opening sentence, "Now when Lot had separated from Abraham . . . ," and comprises then only a promise discourse in which God commands Abraham to survey the land (verse 14) and walk through it (verse 17). But the real content of this scene is the promise discourse. Independent promise scenes are found in 12:7 and 26:24–25.

(b) A promise discourse opens the Abraham cycle (12:1–3) as well as the Jacob/Esau cycle (26:2–5).

(c) A promise discourse has been added secondarily to a narrative in 22:15–18; 26:2–5; 28:13(14)–15; 35:9–13 (P); 15:13–16; 28:3–4 (P); 46:3–4.

(d) A short promise statement has been appended to a promise belonging with the narrative in 16:10 and 21:13.

7. See above, pp. 31–35.

(e) References to a previous promise are found in 18:18–19; 24:7; 32:10–13; 48:3–4 (P).

Thus we can correct what earlier presentations have said about the relationship between the promise motif and the patriarchal narratives. The promise can no longer be termed a theme of the patriarchal narratives (Noth) or a component of most of the narratives (Zimmerli); we find rather that it is an original component of just a few of the patriarchal narratives. Elsewhere—in the vast majority of the texts—it was added during the stage when the ancient narratives were being brought together and elaborated.[8]

To make the same point from the perspective of a historical survey: From Wellhausen to Galling, the promises belong solely to the literary stage; according to Galling, they express "the historico-theological faith of the authors" (*Die Erwählungstraditionen Israels*). Among the followers of Alt (more precisely in Alt's own work), the promises are traced back to the fathers themselves, that is, to the preliterary stage. Since, however, a portion of the promise texts (for example, Gen. 12:1–3) are considered the work of the Yahwist, the question arises about the criteria by which to judge whether a promise belongs to the preliterary or the literary phase. On this point uncertainty reigns; it is therefore necessary to study the individual promises and inquire into their mutual relationship.

THE ORGANIZATION OF THE PROMISES

The history of scholarship has witnessed a consistently more and more precise differentiation of the individual promises. Galling still does not distinguish between the individual promises; what matters to him is that they express the election faith

8. Hoftijzer, *Verheissungen*, and above, pages 2–29. Genesis 26:2–5 is a particularly clear example: the promise does not appear in the two parallels, chapters 12 and 20.

of the authors. For Alt and most other scholars, the really important promises are those of land and descendants, the latter including the promise of a son. In his survey (see above, p. 99),
von Rad adds the promise of a blessing and the promise of a new
relationship with God. The promise of a blessing is defined in
more detail by Wolff (see above), and exhibits a connection
with the promise of increase. Westermann demonstrates the
independence of the promise of a son from the promise of many
descendants. Maag distinguishes the promise of possession of the
land from the promise of new territory or pasturage associated
with transmigration. Finally, there is added the promise of aid
and presence ("I will be with you"), even if it can be called a
promise only with reservations.[9] There are various possibilities
for grouping these promises.

(a) The classification can be undertaken on the plane of
literary criticism, studying the promises in the preliterary period,
in the Yahwist, in the Elohist, and in P. The attempt can then
be made to trace the development of the promises from the earliest to the latest literary sources.[10] Even Hoftijzer is influenced
—albeit unconsciously—by this division when he distinguishes an
El Shaddai group from a Genesis 15 group, for the former is
identical with P, the latter with the earlier sources. This classification on the basis of literary criticism will not suffice, because
the history of tradition of the various promises is too multiform.

(b) The classification can be evaluative, so that, for example,
the promise of the land is given priority (von Rad), and thus
made determinative for the promises as a whole. The promise can
even be identified with the promise of the land (Herrmann).
Lohfink, too, gives priority to the promise of the land, albeit for
a different reason: in Genesis 15 we have the primary narrative

9. It must be noted that "promise" can only be an inexact term for incidents
so designated; Blythin ("The Patriarchs and the Promise," p. 70) rightly points
out that there is no corresponding word in Hebrew.
10. Staerk, Studien; Galling, Die Erwählungstraditionen Israels.

for "the promise of the land as oath," and therefore the promise of the land is primary. Lohfink, however, recognizes the individual significance of the other promises, each with its particular function. Blythin, too, says, "The promise of land is the more prominent aspect of the twofold promise" (p. 64).

(c) It can also be asked what god it is who makes the promises to the fathers. For Alt, it is the God of the fathers in the case of all the promises, for Eissfeldt the Canaanite El. Since in the course of tradition the divine names can easily be changed (as Eissfeldt himself emphasizes), this question can hardly lead to secure conclusions.

(d) If the promise belongs to a narrative, like the promise of a son in Genesis 18, then it belongs to an incident that falls from beginning to end within the patriarchal period itself; those to whom the promise was made experience its fulfillment. In the case of promises that do not belong to a narrative but exist independent of a particular situation, it is quite possible to promise something that the recipients of the promise will not experience, but only later generations. That the writers themselves were aware of this is shown by the added phrase "to you and your seed" or the formulation "to your seed I will give."

This is the most important distinction between the various promises: the promises that will be fulfilled for those who receive them or for their families must be distinguished from those that can only be fulfilled after Israel is a nation. To make this distinction as clear as possible, an ambiguity in the term "promise" must be pointed out.[11] The word "promise" can refer to a transaction between two persons, but it can also refer to what is promised in this transaction, that is, in a sense the result of the transaction. In the latter case the transaction itself is no longer important, but only the content of the promise.

When promise and fulfillment come close together, as in the promise of a son, the understanding of the word as a process or

---

11. For an example of a one-sided understanding of "promise" as the content of what is promised, see F. Baumgärtel, Verheissung (Gütersloh: Bertelmann, 1952).

transaction predominates. When, however, the fulfillment does not take place until centuries after the promise, the transaction fades into the background; now the whole emphasis is on fulfillment and thus on the content of what was once promised and is now fulfilled. In the case of the promises whose fulfillment falls clearly in the period when Israel became a nation, it is probable that they originated later. This is certainly true of the many allusions to the promise of the land in Deuteronomy.

> Behold, I have set the land before you;
> go in and take possession of the land
> which I swore to your fathers, to Abraham, to Isaac, and to Jacob,
> to give to them and to their descendants after them (Deut. 1:8).

But this can also be true in the case of the promises of possession of the land in Genesis 12—50 when those to whom the promise is addressed cannot possibly receive what is promised, that is, when the promise is actually made to later generations. This distinction, it is true, cannot be made with complete assurance in every instance; but in each case it must be asked whether the fulfillment of the promise lies close at hand or far off. It is not just a question of temporal distance, but also whether fulfillment of the promise presupposes a different way of life. When this is the case, it is reasonable to suppose that the promise was formulated from the perspective of this other way of life. This is certainly true for the promise "I will be your God," found only in P, which presupposes the new relationship with God established at Sinai. It holds true also for the promise of increase, to the extent that the similes ("like the stars of heaven") refer clearly to the greatness of the nation of Israel.[12] It holds true for

12. The fact that these comparisons were so formulated from the perspective of Israel is stated thus by Zimmerli: "There is a sharp contrast between the fathers, on the one hand, singled out and separated from their clan, and, on the other hand, the existence of Israel in its fullness as a whole people. In humble, astonished confession, the biblical writers express this in the symbolic figures of the stars . . ." ("Promise and Fulfillment," p. 92). Similarly Blythin, "The Patriarchs and the Promise," page 65.

the promise of possession of the land, to the extent that this promise implies change from a nomadic to a settled way of life. In the case of these promises, we must at least reckon with the possibility that they do not derive from the patriarchal period, but from later stages.[13]

(e) There can be different kinds of fulfillment. In the case of the promise of a son, it is a unique event, the birth of a son. In the case of the promise of increase, it is a gradual growth extending over generations. The former stands in the context of God's deliverance, the latter in the context of his blessing.

(f) It is also important for an understanding of the promises to note whether a promise stands by itself and a specific situation can be recognized to which it is addressed, or whether the promises are accumulated, as in the extended promise discourses. There is a wealth of possibilities for combining various promises.

Promise of a son by itself: 18:1–16
    with increase: 15:1–6; 16:7–12; (21:12–13)
    with blessing: 17:16

Promise of the land by itself: 12:7; 15:7–21; (24:7)
    with increase: 13:14–17; 35:11–13; 48:3–4
    with increase and blessing: 26:2–6; 27:3–4; 28:13–15 (also presence)

Promise of increase by itself: does not occur
    with blessing: 12:1–3; 18:18–19; 22:15–18
    with the land: (see above)
    with a son: (see above)
    with blessing and presence: 26:2–6; (also land) 25:24–25
    with presence: 46:3–4

Promise of blessing by itself: does not occur
    with increase: (see above)

13. See Maag, discussed above on pp. 102–3.

    with increase and presence: 26:24–25
    with increase and presence and the land: 26:2–5; 28:13–15
    with increase and the land: 28:3–4

Promise of aid (presence) by itself: 31:3
    with increase: 46:3–4
    with increase and blessing: 26:24–25
    with increase and blessing and the land: 26:2–6; 28:13–15

Chapter 17 (P) contains an accumulation of all the promises except the promise of presence.

This survey[14] shows the following: The most frequent promise in Genesis 12—50 is the promise of increase; slightly less frequent is the promise of the land. A differing distribution of the promises in the different patriarchal cycles appears at two points: the promise of a son appears only in the Abraham cycle, and the promise of aid (the promise of God's presence) appears only in the Jacob/Esau cycle. This in itself shows that the promises had independent histories.

It is rare to find a promise by itself (see above). Extensive accumulations of promises appear in P (Gen. 17 and 35:9–13) and also outside of P (Gen. 22:15–18; 26:2–5; 28:13–15). Such accumulations definitely indicate a late period.

The promise of a son is most clearly distinct from the others. It appears only by itself or in conjunction with the promise of increase (see above).

The promises of blessing and of increase do not appear by themselves, but only in conjunction with other promises. Both, however, appear frequently together and also in combination with the promise of presence and the promise of the land. They appear in most combinations.

The promise of the land and the promise of increase appear together in three passages, and are combined with the promise of blessing (and presence) in three other passages.

14. See also the survey in von Rad, "Promised Land," pages 79–80.

THE LATER HISTORY OF THE PROMISES

The promises had an extraordinarily long life span. References to the promises, however, are far from uniformly distributed (see above). Among the prophets they appear first in Jeremiah and Ezekiel; in the Psalms they are rare. They are very frequent, however, in Deuteronomy, where the recollection of the promise of the land, given to the fathers, is more frequent than the land promise passages in Genesis 12—50.[15]

For all the references outside Genesis 12—50, however, it holds true that fulfillment does not come for the fathers themselves but for Israel. The later period had no interest in promises that had been fulfilled for the fathers themselves. This proves conclusively that this distinction must also be observed for the promises within Genesis 12—50. We must reckon not only with a prehistory of the promises in the preliterary period (before J, E, and P), but also with a posthistory after the conclusion of the literary works, that is, a continued development of the motif that appears also in later additions and expansions in Genesis 12—50.

It is a typical sign of later expansions when the promises are represented as being a reward for Abraham's obedience. In Genesis 22:15–18, for example, a motivating clause with obvious emphasis is added to the promise: "because you have done this" (v. 16); "because you have obeyed my voice" (v. 18). Here we can recognize clearly the interests of a later period, for which Abraham's obedience provided a prototype for the present (also 18:19; 26:5). This interest is amply attested in the late period. Abraham now becomes the model of obedience and faith. But for the promises that can be assigned with some assurance to the oldest strata, it is in fact characteristic that they are absolute. Any motivation would be inconceivable.[16]

---

15. In his monograph, Hoftijzer devotes chapter 1 to "the material in Exodus, Leviticus, and Numbers,' chapter 3 to "the material in Deuteronomy," and chapter 4 to "the material outside the Pentateuch."

16. Clements (*Abraham and David*, 1967) also stresses the absolute nature of the promise to Abraham.

For a detailed discussion of the later history of the promises, the works of Hoftijzer and Van Seters should be consulted.[17]

SUMMARY

There is not much that can be said of a comprehensive nature about the promises as a whole. They pervade the entire patriarchal history and retain their significance as promises well into the late period of Israel. They are absolute promises, not conditional upon any actions of the patriarchs. They differ from later words of divine favor in that they are given directly to the fathers, without mediator or cultic mediation.

The differences begin with the observation that a small portion of the promises are a genuine component of narratives, while most appear in promise discourses, scenes, additions, and interpolations.

A further difference consists in the fact that some of the promises are conceived as being fulfilled in the patriarchal period, others in the period of Israel's nationhood. With this difference there is often associated the difference that the promises may appear by themselves or in larger accumulations.

Finally, the relationship between promise and fulfillment can vary greatly. The promise of a son is fulfilled in a single event, the promise of increase is a constant process extending over generations.

Thus our study of the promises as a whole comes to the conclusion that each individual promise must be examined to determine its significance and function.

---

17. To the works they cite should be added F. C. Fensham, "Covenant, Promise, and Expectation in the Bible," *Theologische Zeitschrift* 23 (1967): 305–22; H. Gross, "Zum Problem von Verheissung und Erfüllung," *Biblische Zeitschrift* 3 (1959): 3–17; J. Haspecker, "Natur und Heilserfahrung in Altisrael," *Bibel und Leben* 7 (1966): 83–98.

III
The Promises in Detail

THE PROMISE OF A SON

Texts: Genesis 15:2, 3; 16:11; 18:10, 14; (21:1–3); 17:15, 16, 19, 21.

NARRATIVE CONTEXT

In the patriarchal stories we find a promise of which one can say with full assurance that it is intended to take effect for those to whom it is spoken, that it originally belongs to a narrative, and that this narrative originally contained only a single promise: the promise of a son. Its significance has usually been ignored heretofore because it has been subordinated to the promise of many descendants. This is understandable, because in a logical sense the promise of descendants includes the promise of a son, and because the two were linked together at an early stage (15:1–6; 16:7–12; 21:12–13; and the Ugaritic text Krt I K). It can be easily shown, however, that the two promises were originally independent.

The promise of a son belongs from the very outset to a narrative context. It is based on the exigency of childlessness; in this situation the promise is given to solve the problem. The promised event, the birth of a child, alleviates the distress. The promise of a son also occurs elsewhere in the Old Testament as a narrative motif: Judges 13:2–5; 1 Samuel 1; 2 Kings 4:8–17. Its significance extends into the New Testament, where it is determinative for the introduction of the Gospel of Luke (Luke 1–2).

This motif likewise appears in the Ugaritic Krt and Aqht texts, with the same sequence: childlessness—promise of a son—birth of a son. Thus the promise of a son in the patriarchal stories has a clear parallel, attested several times, in roughly contemporary texts from outside Israel but belonging to the same cultural sphere.[18]

The promise of a son is not found throughout Genesis 12—50; it is limited to the Abraham cycle, where, however, it has a dominant importance. The Abraham narrative begins in 11:30 with the motif of the childless mother. The lament of the childless father appears in two variants, verses 2 and 3, in Genesis 15:1–6. The promise of a son is given to the concubine in 16:11 and to Sarah in 18:10, 14. The birth of the child is recounted in 21:1–3. The late recension of P in chapter 17 incorporates and transforms all these motifs.

We see that the sequence of motifs that includes the promise of a son is determinative for the cycle of Abraham narratives; it is a kind of leitmotiv. After the conclusion of the Abraham narratives, however, the motif does not appear again. It will be noted that it is the Abraham narratives that mark the beginning of the patriarchal history. The motif also introduces the narrative in Krt and Aqht, as well as in the Gospel of Luke. One might also cite 1 Samuel 1 in this regard. Now, however, there appears a difference between the promise of a son in the Ugaritic texts and in Genesis 12—25; in the former, there is a complete narrative that leads from the lament of the childless father to the birth of his son, whereas in Genesis 12—25 the sequence of motifs is distributed among several texts. At the beginning, in 11:30, there is the barrenness of Sarah; in 15:2 and 3 there is the lament of childless Abraham; in 15, 16, and 18 the promise of the birth of a son; and chapter 21 the birth. We may conclude that a hypothetical earlier narrative of the promise and birth of a son, encompassing the entire series of motifs, was extant and that the composition of the Abraham narratives, as we have them, drew on these motifs while incorporating many other narratives and narrative motifs.

The hypothesis of a traditio-historical distance between an

18. These parallels are discussed in more detail on pages 165ff. below.

earlier narrative of the promise of a son, no longer extant, and the composition that has been preserved helps to explain several anomalies in the Abraham tradition. Here we shall merely note that the beginning in 11:30 actually leads us to expect that the promise of a son will be addressed to Sarah, such as is addressed to the mother in chapter 16. From chapter 18 we can in fact infer an earlier form of the narrative in which the promise of the birth of Isaac was addressed to Sarah.[19] In all the examples outside Genesis, the promise of a son is addressed to the mother.

It follows that we must reckon with alterations in the texts containing the promise of a son, since the earliest stage of their tradition is no longer extant. This accounts for the variations in the texts containing the promise of a son, which prevent us from inferring a fixed form on their basis.

FEATURES

A few essential features of the promise of a son can still be observed or inferred.

(a) The announcement of the birth of a child comes through a messenger of God. This is uniformly true in 16:11; 18:10, 14; Judges 13:2–5; Luke 1:11–13, 26–37. In 2 Kings 4:16 and Isaiah 7:14, the prophet has taken the place of the messenger. In later passages like Genesis 15:4 and 17:6, it is a different revelation of God. The earliest passages show that the announcement of the birth of a child was an important—if not the most important—function of the mal'ak yhwh.[20] Here an early form of revelation appears side by side with an early promise.

(b) The messenger's announcement to Hagar in Genesis 16:11 has three parts: "Behold, you are with child // and shall bear a son; // you shall call his name Ishmael." Then follows the interpretation of the name. Isaiah 7:14 exhibits precisely the same tripartite form, and it is also preserved in Luke 1:31. This

---

19. See above, page 61.
20. See the articles on angels in such reference works as the *Interpreter's Dictionary of the Bible*.

tripartite announcement (announcement of pregnancy, birth, statement and interpretation of the child's name) probably preserves an ancient form of announcement of the birth of a child. In the case of this form it is certain that the announcement was addressed to the mother.

(c) A different form of the promise of a child is addressed to the father; it appears in 18:10 and 14: "I will surely return to you in the spring // and Sarah your wife shall have a son." The special mark of this announcement is the reference to the date. The same words appear in Elisha's announcement to the Shunammite woman in 2 Kings 4:16. The statement of the date, literally "a year from now about this time," corresponds roughly to the sign associated with the word of divine favor in later periods. The date is something concrete for the person to whom the promise is addressed to hold on to. The second section of Genesis 18:10, literally "Behold, Sarah your wife has a son," could correspond to the message of the birth of a child brought to the father at its birth (Jer. 20:15; Job 3:5). In contrast to 16:11, the naming of the child has been transformed in chapter 18 into an independent motif.

(d) In Genesis 15:4, the promise has undergone major changes. In fact the statement in 15:4 that the offspring of Abraham's own body will be his heir is not really a promise of a son, except by implication. The statement is obviously patterned after Abraham's lament in 15:3; Abraham laments that one of his house slaves will be his heir. The actual lament of childlessness appears in verse 2: "I continue childless!" The natural response would be the direct promise of a son. The placing of the whole emphasis on the heir in God's response to the lament appears to indicate a stage in which the handing on of property, inheritance, was the truly important consideration. It may be asked whether this formulation would have been possible before the period of settlement, when property and its remaining within the family took on such great importance. In any case, Genesis 15:4 represents a later formulation than 16 and 18.

(e) The Priestly promise of a son in Genesis 17 is clearly recognizable as a late modification, presupposing earlier narratives, especially the J material in chapters 16 and 18, and possibly also Genesis 15. In 17:15–16, Abraham is promised that he will also have a son by his wife. In the formulation, the promise of a son is combined with the promise of blessing: "I will bless her, and she shall be a mother of nations." As in Genesis 1, the verb brk refers here to the power of fertility. In verse 16b, the promise of a son is followed immediately by a promise of increase, which is repeated in verses 17–21, in a form much closer to the early form. The motif of laughing in verse 17 shows that P presupposes the narrative of the Yahwist (chapter 18). As in chapter 15, the promise of a son in verse 19 follows the lament of the childless father in verse 18, except that in P the lament has been attenuated and changed into an expression of pious resignation: "Oh that Ishmael might live in thy sight!" The promise "No, but Sarah your wife shall bear you a son" is linked (as in 16:11) with the statement of his name: "and you shall call his name Isaac." Then there follows the promise of a covenant, in line with the tendency of P to accumulate the promises.

That Abraham's wish with respect to Ishmael (v. 18) is also to be fulfilled is stated in verse 20, contrasted once again with the promise, to which the date, likewise deriving from chapter 18, is appended (v. 21): "But I will establish my covenant with Isaac, whom Sarah shall bear to you at this season next year." The addition of the promise of a covenant in verses 19b and 21 shows how P theologizes the promise. It has nothing directly to do with the promise of a son. The covenant, which is to be established with Isaac, not with Ishmael, looks forward already to Israel's special relationship with God established at Sinai.[21]

21. W. Zimmerli, "Sinaibund und Abrahambund," *Theologische Zeitschrift* 16 (1960): 268–80 = his *Gottes Offenbarung, Theologische Bücherei* 19 (München: Kaiser, 1963), pp. 206–16; A. Jepsen, "Berith," *Verbannung und Heimkehr* [Festschrift W. Rudolph] (Tübingen: Mohr, 1961), pp. 161–79; E. Kutsch, "Gesetz und Gnade," *Zeitschrift für die Alttestamentiliche Wissenschaft* 79 (1967): 18–34; C. Westermann, "Gen. 17 und der Bund," *Theologische Literaturzeitung* 101 (1976): 161–70.

(f) The fulfillment of the promise given in chapter 18 is recounted in Genesis 21:1–3. In an earlier form this was probably the conclusion of the narrative of the promise of a son in Genesis 18. The connection with Genesis 18 is underlined several times in 21:1–3 by allusions to the promise. A very surprising fact comes to light when the allusions in verses 1, 2, and 3 are left out: we are left with a report of the birth of the child that does not correspond at all to the promise in Genesis 18, but quite precisely to the promise in Genesis 16:11.

And Yahweh visited Sarah . . .
And Sarah conceived,
and bore Abraham a son in his old age.
And Abraham called the name of his son
whom Sarah bore him, Isaac.

We see that the conclusion in 21:1–3 derives from an earlier narrative of the promise of a son to Abraham (or Sarah) that had contained a formulation of the promise analogous to 16:11.

We conclude that the motifs of the narrative of the promise and birth of a son appear in great multiplicity and variety in the Abraham narratives. It is highly probable that this narrative belongs to the earliest stock of the patriarchal stories, going back to the patriarchal period.[22]

---

22. Others have supported the antiquity of the promise of a son: T. E. Ridenhour, *The Old Testament and the Patriarchal Traditions*, Dissertation, Duke, 1972 (abstract in *Dissertation Abstracts International* 33 [1972/73], p. 6443-A); W. H. Schmidt, *Alttestamentlicher Glaube und seine Umwelt*, Neukirchener Studienbücher 6 (Neukirchen: Neukirchener Verlag, 1968). Mention should also be made of the promise of a son addressed to a king. In the Ugaritic epics of Krt and Aqht, the promise of a son in the present text is addressed to a king (see below, page 169); the promise of a son to a king also appears elsewhere, as is pointed out by H. Cazelles, "Patriarches," *Dictionnaire de la Bible. Supplément* 7 (1966), pp. 144–45: "In Egypt, the promise is given as often to the queen as to the king. . . . At Deir el Bahari and at Luxor, the announcement precedes the conception." The relationship of these promises of a son to the promises of a son in the patriarchal narratives should be investigated further, as well as the promise of a savior king. It is striking that the promise of long life, common in the royal promises, never appears in the patriarchal material.

THE PROMISE OF NEW TERRITORY

Under this heading we must refer at the outset to the works of V. Maag.[23] He places all his emphasis on the nomadic nature of the patriarchal religion and considers transmigration a particularly typical event in the life of nomadic herdsmen: the change to a new and distant pasturage, often reachable only with great hardship. As a modern example, Maag cites a transmigration of the Bakhtiars filmed by Sven Hedin. He sees in this event the original locus of the promise of new pasturage, which means for the tribe deliverance from perishing. It is associated from the outset with the command or instruction to depart and with guidance on the journey ("Hirte," pp. 10, 13, 14). At the same time, Maag distinguishes this promise of new pasturage, associated with transmigration, from the promise of possession of the settled land. "This corresponds to the religio-historical observation that the notion of *possession* of land, like that of national existence, is not one of the primary desiderata of nomadic tribes" ("Malkût," p. 140, n. 2). Behind this distinction stands the criterion of whether a promise is meant to effect something for those to whom it is given or for later generations. The promise of new territory in the context of transmigration addresses a life-or-death question for the nomadic group. Maag also takes into account the additional criterion that the promise of new pasturage is given in a situation of extreme distress (especially "Malkût," p. 138, n. 1), and the fulfillment of the promise means an alleviation of the distress. That such a promise could belong to the patriarchal period has been shown by Maag.

There is a major difficulty, however, with Maag's thesis. The patriarchal history does not contain a single narrative of such a transmigration. If, as Maag says, transmigration is really so typical of the life of nomadic herdsmen, it is natural to assume that at least one narrative mentioning it would have been preserved;

23. See above, page 102.

but this is not the case. One can then ask whether traces at least
of such a narrative have been preserved. Maag finds such traces
above all in Genesis 12:1 ("Hirte," p. 10; "Malkût," p. 138).
He interprets Genesis 12:1–3 as a command to depart and a
promise of new pasturage in the context of transmigration. The
same is true of "Jacob's move from Harran through Transjordan
to the land west of the Jordan" ("Hirte," p. 10). But this latter
is not depicted in the fashion of the transmigration of the Bakhtiars, and whether 12:1–3 can be interpreted in this way is certainly unclear. It is hard to form a conclusion. Maag's thesis
presupposes that possession of land "is not one of the primary
desiderata of nomadic tribes." The majority of scholars assert the
contrary, namely that "fringe nomads," constantly in contact
with the settled region during change of pasturage (transmigration), were in fact intent on settling there. One thing is certain:
the promise of new pasturage in the situation of threatened
famine is fundamentally different from the promise of possession
of settled territory and is more in tune with the nomadic way of
life. As a promise concerned with the alleviation of distress, it
resembles the promise of a son. We must therefore reckon with
the possibility that the patriarchal period was also familiar with
such a promise of new territory. It must be admitted, however,
that the patriarchal narratives have preserved neither a narrative
of a transmigration nor a clearly recognizable promise that would
fit this situation.

But the theory that a transmigration promise can be inferred
behind Genesis 12:1–3, although the passage in its present form
is a composition of the Yahwist, is bolstered by a form-critical
observation. The promise in 12:1–3 follows a command or instruction. Such a combination of commandment and instruction
with a promise can also be presupposed in Exodus 3; it reappears
with the charismatic leaders, where promise also follows instruction. But it also appears in Genesis 12—50 in those passages
where the God of the fathers gives instructions to depart (46:1–3)
or to stay (26:2–3), followed by a promise of presence and aid.

Then an earlier form can be assumed to lie behind the present text of Genesis 12:1-3, containing the instruction to depart for transmigration together with the promise of new pasturage. In this case the promise of possession of the (settled) land must be later; it cannot belong to the earliest stock of the patriarchal promises. We may leave open the possibility that there were intermediate forms representing a transition from the one to the other. It is not impossible that the phrase in Deuteronomy 26:5, "A perishing Aramean was my father,"[24] points to a transmigration and its accompanying promise.[25]

THE PROMISE OF AID

Texts: Genesis 26:3; 26:24; 28:15; (20); 31:3; 32:10; 46:3; (48:15, 21; 50:24).

None of the texts belongs to the Abraham cycle; the promise of God's presence is restricted to Genesis 26—50. In 26:3, 24, its recipient is Isaac; elsewhere it is Jacob. Here we can recognize a deliberate structural feature. While the promise of a son appears only in the Abraham cycle, the promise of God's presence appears only in 26—50. Just as the former motif permeates 12—25, the latter permeates 26—50. Maag was the first to draw attention to this promise; it is not included among the promises by earlier studies. It is also not the announcement of an event in the sense of the promise of a son, which is then fulfilled in the birth of a son. It is also not a promise in the sense that one could speak of the object of the promise, as in the case of the promise of the land or the promise of increase. However, that the

24. See Seebass, *Der Erzväter Israel*, p. 4.
25. The common expression "God brought us out" (yṣ', hiphil) also suggests a combination of instruction to depart with a promise; if one asks how God's "bringing out" is understood, it probably means: God gave instruction to depart, associated with a promise. See also Seebass, *Der Erzväter Israel*, page 32: "Maag rightly emphasizes (p. 140, n. 2) that the transmigration of a nomadic group is inconceivable without a divine promise."

statement "I will be with you" occurs in combination with other promises, as in 26:2-5, is sufficient for us to include it in our study of the promise texts. It might be called an assurance or a pledge.

The promise of God's presence shares with the first two promises studied here the characteristic that it is meant for those to whom it is addressed, not later generations. Maag sees this promise in loose association with transmigration: it is the shepherd God who promises escort. In any case, the passages indicate clearly that God's presence is always promised for a journey. Therefore, it can be associated with a command or instruction to depart (46:1-3) or to remain (26:1-3) or to return (31:3). These two observations taken together—the fulfillment of the promise for those to whom it is given and its association with an instruction although always related to a journey—argue for an origin of this promise in the patriarchal period.

Another observation could argue the contrary: this promise is in no way limited to the patriarchal period but is found in all periods of the Old Testament writings. It has been studied in the entire range of its occurrences by H. D. Preuss ("Ich will mit dir sein," Zeitschrift für die Alttestamentliche Wissenschaft 80 [1968]: 139-73). Preuss examines the hundred or so passages, classified according to whether the expression is used as a promise and pledge given by God; a promise, pledge, request, or wish on the part of a person; or a human observation, concluding, "It is noteworthy that the earliest texts use it predominantly as a pledge before or during a journey" (p. 144), even when it is spoken by a human being (p. 147) or used as an assertion (p. 151). "The patriarchal stories (apart from the story of Joseph) are one of the focal points of the formula. Here we find four promises by God, two pledges by men, and five assertions . . . , altogether 11 out of some 93 occurrences" (p. 152). "Within these family stories of nomadic character, the God of those to whom the formula is addressed appears as a deity who accompanies, escorts, protects, and leads. Here this promise and this formula have their original concrete meaning as elements of nomadic thought and belief" (p. 153).

Study of all the occurrences of the formula in the Old Testament (listed on pp. 141–51) confirms that it is not only possible but probable that the promise of God's presence reaches back to the patriarchal period. Preuss then examines a whole series of ancient Near Eastern texts searching for parallels. He finds only a few similar texts, with no well attested similarity of usage, and concludes, "It is safe to say . . . that the formula of the presence of a deity with an individual or group appears to have been much less common in the ancient Near East than within Israel and its Old Testament" (p. 170). The typically Israelite aspect of this formula consists in "its original locus being in nomadic piety" (p. 170).

D. Vetter (*Jahwes mit-Sein als Ausdruck des Segens*, Arbeiten zur Theologie 5 [Stuttgart: Calwer, 1971], pp. 6–9) also examines "the use of the formula in the patriarchal narratives." He agrees with Preuss that the formula has a specifically nomadic character. "The patriarchal stories employ the formula only in the context of someone's journey . . . . The realm of nomadism therefore appears to have been the specific situation for talk of God's accompanying presence" (p. 9). Vetter, however, argues against including the statement among the promises. "Yahweh's presence is not announced or promised for a later date, but rather is stated as a fixed datum, . . . it refers to a constant action on the part of God" (p. 8). He rightly notes, "Nowhere does Yahweh's presence refer to a single unique event;" but if God's presence means protection during a journey, it does indeed refer to a series of events. And if it is assured before departure, although it does not refer to a single later date, it does refer to a series of later dates: the perilous situations to be encountered on the journey. God's accompanying presence during the journey is constant in that it is not a momentary event like the alleviation of a need. God will be with Jacob from the moment he departs until he reaches his goal (28:20); his presence means constant protection and care along the way. Since, however, this presence can be assured before departure, it is in fact reasonable to find it in 26:2–5 and 26:24–25 in a series of several promises.

This usage must be distinguished from the use of the formula by others to confirm someone's success, wealth, or superiority, a use found clearly in Genesis only in the Joseph narrative (39:2; 39:28). In 12—36 this same situation is termed a blessing; 24:1, for example, states, ". . . and Yahweh had blessed him in all things." A transitional stage appears in 31:5, 42; 32:11, 13, where the accompanying presence of God approximates a blessing.

In conclusion, we can say of the promise of God's presence and aid on a journey that it probably goes back to the patriarchal period and was deliberately associated with the section of the patriarchal stories in which the journeyings of one of the fathers constitute a major component of the narrative.

THE PROMISE OF THE LAND

Texts: Genesis 12:7; 13:14–15; 13:17; 15:7–21; 17:8; 24:7; 26:3, 4; 28:4, 13; 35:12; 48:4; 50:24. Outside of Genesis 12—50: Exodus 13:5, 11; 32:13; 33:1; Numbers 11:12; 14:16, 23; 32:11; Deuteronomy 1:8, 35; 4:31; 6:10, 18, 23; and thirteen additional passages.

THE DISTRIBUTION OF THE TEXTS

The texts show that all the emphasis is on the promise of the land made to Abraham. This is shown by 15:7–21, the great central narrative in which the promise of the land is represented as an oath on the part of Yahweh. It is shown also by the scene in 13:14–17, in which the promise to Abraham is associated with the ritual of conveyance, and by the "narrative allusion" 12:7, in which the promise stands by itself, as well as in the reference to the promise in 24:7. The traditionists were so convinced that

Abraham was the real recipient of the promise of the land that in the majority of passages in Genesis 26—50 they characterize the promise of the land given to Jacob as a renewal of the promise given to Abraham: 26:3, 4; 50:24; also in P: 28:4; 35:12. An independent promise of the land to Jacob appears only in 28:13, where, however, the God who gives the promise introduces himself as "the God of Abraham your father." This promise to Jacob differs from the promise to Abraham in that it is spoken at a sanctuary. Aside from 28:13, it appears in the non-P portions of 26—50 in the introductory promise 26:2–5 (3c, 4b) and in the final words of Joseph (50:24), which constitute the transition to the exodus. The other passages (28:4; 35:12; 48:4) belong to P; 28:4 and 35:12 expressly emphasize that "the land of your sojournings which God gave to Abraham" is pledged to the descendants of Jacob. It is noteworthy that the great P promise discourse in chapter 17 includes the promise of the land in 17:8 as a secondary addition. The emphasis here is on the promise of a son and descendants.

THE CONTEXT OF THE PROMISE OF THE LAND

We must first distinguish the instances where the promise of the land is a component of a narrative from those where it is not. The narrative in 15:7–21 has the promise of the land as its only subject; the promise has here been shaped into a narrative.[26] Like 15:1–6, 15:7–21 is a promise narrative in the sense that God's oath, in which he guarantees Abraham the gift of the land, has been cast in the form of a narrative. Genesis 28:13 is a component of a narrative in a totally different sense: it is a word from God revealed to Jacob in a dream at a sacred site, and the promise is linked with this setting by a relative clause: "the land on which you lie." Genesis 13:14–17 is not an independent narrative but a scene appended to the narrative of Lot's separation from Abraham. The promise is linked with two commands

26. Lohfink, *Die Landesverheissung als Eid*, calls it an "artificial narrative."

(verses 14b and 17). Genesis 12:7 can also be called a scene, where the promise is followed by construction of an altar.

The promise of the land without an accompanying action appears only in 26:2–5 (verses 3b, 4b) and in P (17:8; 28:4; 48:4). The other passages involved are an allusion (24:7) and a transitional link (50:24).

This survey shows that, apart from P, the promise of the land appears primarily as part of a narrative or scene. It appears in promise discourses only in texts that are certainly late. None of the narratives, however, recounts a sequence of events that includes the promises as a necessary element, as in the transmigration promise. We may conclude that the promise of the land is associated primarily with an action but that a secure place in the earliest stratum is not demonstrable.[27]

A different view is presented by the studies of Seebass (1966) and Lohfink (1967). Seebass considers 28:13 to be the fundamental passage, since here it is not yet possession of the entire land that is promised, but only possession of the land associated with the sanctuary of Bethel. Lohfink finds the fundamental passage in 15:7–21, because for him "the promise as an oath" is the earliest passage containing the promise of the land, from which all the others derive. Seebass's hypothesis is contradicted by the uncertainty as to whether 28:13 belongs to the earliest ascertainable form of 28:10ff., as well as by the fact that the sanctuary narrative probably does not belong to the earliest stratum of the patriarchal narratives. Lohfink's hypothesis is contradicted by the implication of his explanation that the oath reinforces a promise of the land given earlier, so that this earlier promise without the oath should be the subject of inquiry. In addition, it is impossible to deny that the other texts in which

27. See also L. A. Snijders, "Genesis XV, the Covenant with Abraham," *Oudtestamentische Studien* 12 (1958): 27. This view is also supported by the important observation of Blythin ("The Patriarchs and The Promise," p. 67) that the element of promise does not appear in the earliest formulation of the credo in Deuteronomy 26: "The transition from the 'ărām 'ōbēd to the populous nation expresses amazement at the unexpected rather than a declaration of the fulfillment of promise."

the promise of the land is termed an oath are predominantly late texts, above all the many passages in Deuteronomy.[28]

THE LINGUISTIC FORM OF THE PROMISE

In the case of the promise of the land, we can speak of a fixed linguistic form or even of a formula. In 12:7 and 24:7 the wording is identical: "To your descendants I will give this land." The same words are used in 15:18, except that the verb is in the perfect. All other occurrences are so similar that we must presuppose a fixed idiom, determined by the verb *ntn*, "give," which is common to all the passages. This word characterizes the promise of the land. It is intended as a gift, a transfer, or a conveyance, and is so termed. This raises a difficulty: what is meant by the statement "I (Yahweh) give this land to you (Abraham)"? Yahweh cannot give or convey it to Abraham, because it will not and cannot be Abraham's during his lifetime. The traditionists saw this problem and therefore used the formula "to you and your descendants" (13:15; 28:13) or just "your descendants" (12:7; 24:7; 15:18). Here the precise expression is "your descendants"; the form "you and your descendants" serves a transitional function.[29] If we take the formula "to your descendants I will give this land" as our starting point, it says quite clearly that, although the promise of the land is given to Abraham, it promises him something that he is not to receive, but rather his descendants. This form therefore presupposes some distance from the patriarchal period; such a formulation is possible only after the patriarchal period.

The verb *ntn*, "give," is actually inappropriate in the context of this temporal distance, since it refers to conveyance in the present. Also inappropriate to this temporal distance is the sol-

28. J. Hoftijzer, *Die Verheissungen an die drei Erzväter*, part III; N. Lohfink, *Die Landesverheissung als Eid*, pp. 15–17. H. C. White, "The Divine Oath in Genesis," *Journal of Biblical Literature* 92 (1973): 165–79, sees an oath ceremony of Semitic nomads behind the promise narratives.
29. A study by R. Rendtorff of the linguistic form of the promise of the land is to appear soon.

emn act of conveyancing depicted in 13:14–17, as well as the fact that apart from P the promise of the land is associated with an action. An act like that in 13:14ff. is more suggestive of conveyancing than of a promise. Only the temporal distance turns the act into a promise; if we bracket out this distance, then we are left with a solemn conveyancing that is legally in force the moment it is performed. Thus Horst (*Gottes Recht*, Theologische Bücherei 12 [München: Kaiser, 1961]) says with reference to this passage that "personal progress through the length and breadth of the property was one of the forms of taking possession." That the formula is in fact used for the conveyancing of property between two individuals is shown by Genesis 48:22. Jacob-Israel bequeaths a piece of land to Joseph with the words "I give you Shechem." And in the solemn oath of 15:18 we find: "to your descendants I give this land." It is obviously the same formula, changed to fit the situation. P can also use the formula in 28:4—"the land . . . which God gave to Abraham." The solemn form of conveyancing appears once again in Deuteronomy 1:8.[30] We may conclude, therefore, that the promise of the land as variously formulated is based on a familiar formula used for conveying land, as the ritual alluded to in 13:14–17 still suggests.

This conclusion is in line with the distinction proposed by Maag between a promise of new pasturage for deliverance from famine and the promise of possession of the land, set in a time of transition from nomadic to settled life. In this case the promise of settled territory would not have originated in the patriarchal period but rather in the period when *possession* of the land had become a vital question for the tribes beginning to settle in Canaan. It is likely that the promise of possession of the land presupposed the ancient promise of land in its nomadic form, and that there were transitional forms.[31]

30. See above, pp. 126–27.
31. See the cautious remarks of S. Herrmann, *A History of Israel in Old Testament Times* (Philadelphia: Fortress, 1975). It is nevertheless an open question whether the patriarchs themselves already lived and acted in the prospect of a future society.

LATER HISTORY OF THE PROMISE OF THE LAND

The conclusion of the patriarchal history places the motif of the promise of the land once more in the mouth of the dying Joseph (50:24).

> I am about to die; but God will visit you,
> and bring you up out of this land to the land
> which he swore to Abraham, to Isaac, and to Jacob (RSV).

This statement marks the transition from the patriarchal history to the history of the exodus. As Joseph dies, he prophesies the exodus from Egypt; the exodus promise of Exodus 3:7 is linked here with the promise of the land given to the fathers.[32] In this statement we are told that the fulfillment of the promise given to the fathers Abraham, Isaac, and Jacob is seen in the gift of the land of Canaan to Israel as it comes up out of Egypt. This prophecy of Joseph as he dies cannot have come into being until after the patriarchal traditions were already linked with the exodus traditions. If the promise of the land to the fathers serves here to connect the history of the people of Israel with the history of the patriarchs, it cannot date from the patriarchal period.

In Genesis 50:24, the promise of the land to the fathers is termed an oath: "The land, which he swore to Abraham. . . ." Apart from this passage, the promise of the land as an oath sworn to the fathers or to Abraham appears in Genesis 12—50 only in Genesis 26:3b and 24:7, both late passages, and the oath ceremony in 15:7–21, discussed above. But the center of gravity of this concept is the large group of passages (twenty-one) in Deuteronomy in which the promise of the land to the fathers took on the function of legitimizing or sanctioning something that happened long after the patriarchal period; this function is betrayed by the stereotyped usage of the word "swear": Yahweh swore that he would give the land to the descendants of the fathers. An

---

32. See the discussion on page 120 above and von Rad, *Genesis*, page 428; Noth, *A History of Pentateuchal Traditions*, pages 61–62.

oath becomes necessary when its intended guarantee of a statement is necessary. This uncertainty corresponds to the situation before and during the conquest, that is, precisely the situation addressed by Deuteronomy's stylized address of Moses before the crossing of the Jordan. There is no reason to assume that the conditions leading to the oath formulation of the promise were not present until the late period, around the time of the Exile (Hoftijzer, p. 39; Van Seters). What it suggests is not a situation "in which the existence of the nation was imperilled" (Hoftijzer) but the situation during the conquest of constant uncertainty whether the land would really be Israel's land.

A detailed study of the later history of the promise of the land would have to start with its transformed function in the period of the conquest, examining first the relationship between the promise of the land to the fathers and the promise of the land to the exodus group (Exod. 3:7).[33]

THE PROMISE OF INCREASE

Texts: Genesis 12:1–3; 13:16; 15:5; 16:10; 17:5, 6, 16, 20; 18:18; 21:13, 18; 22:17, 18; 26:2–5, 24, 25; 28:3, 14; 32:13; 35:11; 46:3; (47:27); 48:4, 16, 19. Outside Genesis 12—50: (Exod. 1); Exodus 32:10; Numbers 14:12; Deuteronomy 1:10, 11; 6:3; 13:18; 15:6; Isaiah 51:2; Nehemiah 9:23.

THE PROMISE OF INCREASE AND THE PROMISE OF A SON

That the promise of a son and the promise of increase are both independent promises has already been shown in our discussion of the former. Like the promise of a son itself, the combination of the promise of a son and the promise of increase occurs only in the Abraham cycle. The connection between the two is particularly clear and impressive in Genesis 15:4, 5. The response to

33. On the later history of the promise of the land, see Hoftijzer *Die Verheissungen an die drei Erzväter*, Lohfink, *Die Landesverheissung als Eid*, and J. Van Seters, "Confessional Reformulation in the Exilic Period," *VT* 22 (1972): 448–59.

the lament of the childless father (vv. 2, 3) is the promise of a son, with its formulation changed to fit the situation. The beginning of verse 5 introduces a new scene: "And he brought him outside. . . ." This fresh beginning shows clearly that the original independence of the two promises is still sensed. Likewise, however, the sequence of verses 4 and 5 shows that the promise of innumerable descendants is understood as an amplification of the promise of a son; and it is clear that it is just this amplification that has present significance for the descendants of Abraham in the land of promise, as the late echo of this promise of increase in Isaiah 51:2 still directly reflects. "Look to Abraham your father and to Sarah who bore you; for when he was but one I called him, and I blessed him and made him many" (RSV).

The original independence of the two promises is still apparent also in Genesis 16:10–12,[34] where the promise of a son and the promise of increase still stand in parataxis, both introduced by the same expression: "And the angel of Yahweh said to her. . . ." It can be seen that the promise of increase was added during the growth of the narrative. The situation differs in 21: 12–13, 17–18, because Ishmael has already been born and thus there is no longer any room for the promise of a son. Here too, however, we can still see that the two promises were originally independent.

From this group of passages in which the promise of a son and the promise of increase occur together, we can conclude that the original independence of the two promises can still be seen but that the two were combined relatively often, obviously in a very early stage of the tradition.[35]

The Linguistic Form of the Promise of Increase

It is a striking fact that this promise more than all the rest makes use of fixed idioms, repeated almost or totally verbatim in

34. See above, page 134.
35. The two promises are also combined in the Ugaritic Krt; see above, page 133.

many passages. The language of the promise of increase often approaches poetry, as is shown by the many pairs of synonyms, the poetic similes, and the exaggerated mode of expression.

The promise of increase makes constant use of the verb rbh, "become many." "I will so greatly multiply [cause to become many] your descendants . . ." (16:10; also 22:17; 26:4; 26:24). The formulation of P is different, where we usually find "make fruitful and multiply" together: "I will . . . make him fruitful and multiply him . . ." (17:20; also 28:3; 35:11; 48:4; 27:27 [fulfillment]). In 17:6 we find rbh alone.[36]

Especially typical for the promise of increase are the comparisons to the stars of heaven: 15:5; 22:17; 26:4; also Exodus 32:13; Deuteronomy 1:10; 10:22; 28:62; Nehemiah 9:23; to the sand of the sea: 22:17; 32:12; also Isaiah 10:22; 48:19; to the dust of the earth: 13:16; 28:14. Countlessness is emphasized in 13:16; 15:5; 16:10; 32:13.

In all the previously mentioned passages containing the promise of increase, all that is promised is a great number of descendants; the reference is to descendants in the realm of family or clan. Formulated in this fashion, the promise must go back to a process that takes place within the family and does not extend into another form of society. But the promise of increase has a variant in which we can observe the transition from family to nation. One of the fathers is promised: "I will make you a great nation" (12:2; 17:20; 18:18; 21:13, 18; 46:3; also Exod. 32:10; Num. 14:12). It will be noted that the concept of greatness first appears with the mention of the nation. Only here does greatness become a desideratum. In all these passages, "great nation" is a fixed concept; greatness inheres in the nation. This is true also in the two passages where the same promise is made to Moses, Exodus 32:10 and Numbers 14:12. This promise is given while Israel is well on its way to becoming a nation, but the same applies

---

36. A. S. Kapelrud, "Fruchtbarkeit," in Biblisch-historisches Handwörterbuch, vol. I (Göttingen: Vandenhoeck, 1962–67), pp. 503f.; M. Oliva, "Las revelaciones a los patriarcas en la historia sacerdotal," Biblica 35 (1974): 1–14.

already in the passages where Abraham (12:2; 18:18), Ishmael (16:10; 21:13, 18), and Jacob (46:3) are promised that they will become great nations. The clearest passage is 12:2, in the introduction to the patriarchal history of the Yahwist; the statement is universally interpreted to mean that the Yahwist here has in prospect the greatness of Israel in the early monarchic period.[37] This variant of the promise of increase thus clearly extends beyond the way of life of the fathers; probably, therefore, as is generally assumed in the case of 12:2, it is a product of the settled period.

This promise takes on even more massive form in P. A clear tendency toward exaggeration can be noted. Abraham will become not just a great nation, but nations (17:16), a company of nations (28:3; 48:4; 35:11), the father of a multitude of nations (17:5). "Kings of nations shall come forth from him" (17:6, 16; 35:11; 17:20 [princes from Ishmael]). In these passages, which appear in great number in P, the purpose is obviously to exalt Abraham, to celebrate in him the greatness of the people of Israel, and to look back over the history of its kings, which is now in the past. Here the object is the nation as an organized state. For this variant of the promise of increase, which refers so unmistakably to Israel's history, to have come into being during the patriarchal period itself is almost inconceivable.[38]

Promise of Increase Linked with Blessing

In many passages the promise of increase is linked with a blessing or the promise of a blessing: 12:2; 17:16, 20; 22:17; 26:4; 26:24; 28:3; 32:13; 35:9–11; 48:3, 4; (48:16); also Isaiah 51:2. This combination of the promise of increase with the verb brk in so many passages is striking. About half the passages belong to P (17:16, 20; 28:3; 35:9, 11; 48:3, 4); two are literarily shaped

---

37. For example, W. Zimmerli, "Promise and Fulfillment"; G. von Rad, *Genesis*; H. W. Wolff, "The Kerygma of the Yahwist"; H. Seebass, *Der Erzväter Israel*, page 3.

38. M. Oliva, "Las revelaciones"; W. Zimmerli, "Sinaibund."

poems (12:2 and 26:3, 4); two occur in a promise discourse (22: 17; 26:24); and 32:13 is an allusion to a promise in the Prayer of Jacob. All of these passages point to a late origin; it would be natural to conclude that the promises of increase and blessing were not combined until the late period. Such a conclusion is contradicted, however, by the fact that 48:16 (generally ascribed to the Elohist), a blessing pronounced by Jacob upon Ephraim and Manasseh, contains the same combination of blessing and increase.

> The God who . . . bless the lads;
> . . . and let them grow into a multitude in the midst of the earth.

Here, in a blessing given by one person to another, increase is the outcome of the blessing. This circumstance suggests that the combination of promise of increase with promise of blessing goes back to the combination of blessing and increase in the act of pronouncing a blessing. This possibility must be pursued.

THE ORIGIN OF THE PROMISE OF INCREASE

A whole series of further observations suggests that the act of blessing in its various forms is the origin of the promise of increase. This is already suggested by the fact that the pair "be fruitful/multiply" derives from God's blessing upon his creation in Genesis 1, so that P accordingly can term the promise of increase a blessing in 48:3, 4. This association is demonstrated with certainty by the fact that most of the terminology used to describe the increase appears in acts of blessing where one individual blesses another. Besides 48:16, increase also appears as a component of a blessing in 24:60, a blessing formula that is certainly older than the narrative in chapter 24.

> Our sister, be the mother of thousands of ten thousands;
> and may your descendants possess the gate of those who hate them!

153

The second part of this blessing is incorporated almost verbatim in the promise of increase in 22:17. The statement "I will make your name great" in 12:2 recalls 48:16: "Bless the lads, and in them let my name be perpetuated, and the name of my fathers Abraham and Isaac." The variant form of the promise, "I will make you a great nation," has an analogue in the Blessing of Jacob: "He also shall become a people, and he also shall be great" (48:19). The following sentence contains the expression "and his descendants shall become a multitude of nations," which is incorporated in P's promise of increase in 28:3 and 48:4. Finally, there is the extension of the promise of blessing (and increase): "By you all the families of the earth will bless themselves" (12:3; see also 18:18; 22:18; 26:4; 28:14) in the Blessing of Jacob (48:20):

> So he blessed them that day, saying,
> "By you Israel will pronounce blessings,
> saying, 'God make you as Ephraim and Manasseh' " (RSV).

When all the expressions used in the promise of increase have been shown to occur in blessings pronounced by one person upon another, it clearly follows that the promise of increase is based on the language and terminology of blessing. In the early period such blessing formulas had a rhythmical poetic form, as shown, for example, by Genesis 24:60. This explains the stereotyped idioms of the promise of increase, the language that is close to poetry, the exaggeration, the frequent occurrence of the same words, and the word pairs.[39]

It may even be possible to specify the origin of the promise of increase more precisely. In the early period, blessings could be given on many occasions, especially when someone was dying or when a member was about to leave the family, as in the case of a

---

39. The origin of the promise of increase from blessing is also seen by Blythin, "The Patriarchs and the Promises," pages 70ff. The connection between the two is also mentioned by A. Murtonen, "The Use and Meaning of the Words lebārēk and berākāh in the Old Testament," Vetus Testamentum 9 (1959): 158–77; and G. Wehmeier, Der Segen im Alten Testament, Theologische Dissertationen 6 [Basel: Reinhardt, 1970].

daughter at her marriage. This is the situation in Genesis 24:60 where the brothers send their sister Rebecca away with a blessing. But the locus of a marriage blessing can also be the wedding celebration. An example is found in the Krt text (cited from Aistleitner's translation). In III K II 1–10, the gods enter the house of Keret for a wedding celebration. Aliyan Baal calls on El to bless Keret (11–16). K II 17–28, continued in K III 1–16, contains the blessing. In 24–31 we read, "Your wife shall bear you seven sons and eight daughters. . . ." This shows that the promise of increase has its origin in the blessing, in particular the marriage blessing.

WISH AND PROMISE

This origin explains an essential peculiarity of the promise of increase. The wish for many descendants, as found in Genesis 24:60 or 48:16, cannot find its fulfillment in a single event, but only in a gradual process of growth extending over generations. This is fulfillment of a different sort than that of the promise of a son, which finds its fulfillment in a single event. But the promises themselves are also different in each case. The promise that addresses a need and pledges alleviation of the need is different from a promise that has nothing to do with alleviation of a need but rather promises further successful development. The promise arising out of the blessing corresponds to the wish that expresses the wish for some positive development. Only thus can we account for the exaggerated images that are characteristic of the promise of increase.[40]

THE PROMISE OF BLESSING

It is not necessary to list the texts again at this point; they have been mentioned in the sections dealing with the promise of increase linked with blessing and occasionally in the preceding sec-

40. In Exodus 1, the increase of the people in Egypt is an introductory motif of the exodus account. The relationship of this motif to that of the promise of increase in Genesis 12—50 deserves further study.

tions. We arrive at the surprising fact that the only text remaining for an independent promise of blessing is Genesis 12:1–3. Here, too, the promise of blessing is linked with the promise of increase; but all the other promises are subordinated to the promise of blessing. In all other texts, the promise of blessing is explicated or elaborated through the promise of increase. This observation confirms the special status and function of Genesis 12:1–3, a literary composition of the Yahwist to introduce the patriarchal history and at the same time form a bridge from the primal history to the patriarchal history. The Yahwist here framed a theological construct of far-reaching importance, by taking the ahistorical blessing and transforming it into a historical concept: the promise of a blessing, looking toward the future.[41] But this transformation of blessing into a historical concept presupposes that, with this promise of blessing to Abraham, the Yahwist is pointing ahead beyond the patriarchal period to the history of the people of Israel, indeed, that he uses this promise to link the patriarchal period with the period of Israel's national history.[42]

This observation confirms, however, that this promise of blessing, framed so deliberately to mark the beginning of a new section, is a historical concept belonging to the historical period; it cannot belong to the patriarchal period. But the blessing on which both the promise of blessing and the promise of increase are based, whose language has been turned into a promise, can easily belong to the patriarchal period.

BLESSING AS INCREASE OF POSSESSIONS

That blessing in the patriarchal period still retains a prehistoric significance is shown by a group of texts stating that one of the fathers is blessed (by God). This is said of Abraham only in the story of Rebecca. At the beginning of this narrative we are

41. This theme has been developed especially by H. W. Wolff, "Kerygma," page 50, and C. Westermann, Blessing, and also in "Way of the Promise," pages 237f.

42. This point has been discussed extensively by von Rad and Wolff.

told, "Yahweh had blessed Abraham in all things," a theme taken up again in 24:35. Abraham's servant is greeted, "Come in, O blessed of Yahweh" (24:31). At the transition from the Abraham to the Isaac narratives, we read in 25:11, "After the death of Abraham God blessed Isaac his son." Isaac's wealth is explained in 26:12–14: "Yahweh blessed him." The same thing is stated by others in 26:28, 29. The same is said of Jacob in the Jacob/Laban narrative (30:27, 30, 43; [32:11]). None of these passages is in the context of a promise; none contains an explicit promise of a blessing. But that is just what is surprising. The blessing that takes effect in progeny was transformed into a promise of a blessing, but not the blessing that takes effect in the increase of possessions or revenue. The dominant mode in the latter case is statement of fact. Either the narrator (24:1, 35; 25:11; 26:12–14; 30:43) or the conversational partner (24:31; 26:28, 29; 30:27, 30; 32:11) states that someone is blessed. These statements illustrate the original concept of blessing: it is the power of fertility and success. The effect of a blessing can be perceived in the present; it is there or it is not there, but it cannot be placed in prospect for a later time.[43]

EXTENSIONS

Besides the promise of increase (v. 2a) and the promise of future greatness (v. 2b), the promise of blessing in 12:1–3 contains two extensions.

> I will bless those who bless you,
> and him who curses you I will curse (3a).

The Yahwist makes this statement refer to Israel: Israel's friends will be Yahweh's friends, Israel's enemies will be Yahweh's enemies.[44] "The words echo formulas of ancient Near Eastern treaties," Vriezen says, citing a sentence in a Ugaritic

---

43. On blessing as material prosperity, see Murtonen, Wehmeier (note 39).
44. T. C. Vriezen, "Bemerkungen zu Genesis 12:1–7," in *Symbolae Biblicae et Mesopotamicae*, Festschrift F. M. T. Böhl (Leiden: Brill, 1973), pp. 380–91.

vassal treaty between Suppiluliuma and Niqmadu: "To the enemy of my lord I am an enemy, and to the friend of my lord I am a friend." Even closer, however, is the parallel in Genesis 27:29 and Numbers 24:9.

Cursed be everyone who curses you,
and blessed be everyone who blesses you.

This parallel shows that this extension, too, derives from a blessing spoken by a person. Here, too, the transformation into a promise is secondary.[45]

The same is true of the other extension in verse 3b: "And by you all the families of the earth will bless themselves." This extension appears frequently; besides the present passage, it is found (niphal or hithpael) in 18:18; 22:18; 26:4; 28:14. It, too, appears in a blessing given by one person to another:

By you men will bless themselves in Israel, saying,
"God make you as Ephraim and as Manasseh" (48:20, emended).

This extension of a blessing survived in the praise of the king.

May men bless themselves by him,
all nations call him blessed (Ps. 72:17).

The two parallels in Genesis 48:20 and Psalm 72:17 make the sense of the extension clear. The blessing that is wished for someone is to take effect in such a way that even those distant in space or time will mention his name and speak of his blessedness when wishing someone good fortune and blessing: "God make you as . . . ."[46]

---

45. On the relationship between the two passages and the various details, see W. Schottroff, Der altisraelitische Fluchspruch, Wissenschaftliche Monographien zum Alten und Neuen Testament 30 (Neukirchen: Neukirchener Verlag, 1969), with index of passages.

46. On this extension of the promise of blessing, see H. Gunkel, Genesis (Göttingen: Vandenhoeck & Ruprecht, ⁷1966); von Rad, Genesis; Wolff, "Kerygma," pages 51–52; and especially J. Schreiner, "Segen für die Völker in der Verheissung an die Väter," Biblische Zeitschrift, NF 6 (1962): 1–31. Schreiner traces the usage back to a Jerusalem temple tradition.

This shows that the statement is an extension of a blessing wish; in this case, too, it is clear that the wish represents the original form, the promise a secondary derivation.[47]

THE PROMISE OF
A COVENANT

This promise appears only in P, and only in Genesis 17:7–8.

And I will establish my covenant between . . .
to be God to you and to your descendants after you.

Similar expressions appear in Genesis 9:9 and Exodus 6:7. We may compare Deuteronomy 29:10–13:

You stand this day all of you before Yahweh your God . . .
that you may enter into the sworn covenant of Yahweh your
God . . .
that he may establish you this day as his people,
and that he may be your God, as he promised you,
and as he swore to your fathers, to Abraham . . . .

We are not dealing here with a promise in the true sense; the only reason for mentioning the passage is that it appears in P in the great promise discourse, Genesis 17. By it, P intends to link the promise to Abraham with the establishment of the relationship between the God Yahweh and Israel at the exodus from Egypt and at Sinai. The statement is very important for P because nothing is said of a covenant made at Sinai. For P there can be only the two covenants with Noah and with Abraham, because there are only two partners with which God can establish his covenant: humankind (Genesis 9) and God's people (Gene-

---

47. "I will make your name great" could be termed a third extension. That it is based on a wish for a blessing on the king is shown by Psalm 72:17 and the hymn to Iddindagan of Isin: see A. Falkenstein, *Sumerische und akkadische Hymnen und Gebete* (Zürich: Artemis, 1953), pp. 120–23. See also the other wishes for kings cited by Cazelles, "Patriarches," pp. 144–45.

sis 17). God's relationship with his people begins with Abraham, who embodies Israel to a much greater degree for P than for the early sources. Therefore we hear the "covenant formula" in 17:7, 8, 19, as in Deuteronomy 29:10–13, where, however, its two parts are mentioned. But these sentences are not a promise of the future covenant: the covenant cannot be promised, it can only be entered into or established. It follows, therefore, that these sentences are the work of P and cannot be based on any tradition going back to the patriarchal period.

It is possible, however, that the statement "I will be your God" is based on the formulation of an oath that promises to serve the God who delivers from distress. We may compare the oath of Jacob at Bethel:

> If God will be with me, and will keep me . . .
> then Yahweh shall be my God (28:20–21).

P could have transformed this statement from oral tradition into an oath. This would be analogous to a similar transformation in the case of the promise of increase.

In its later history, the promise can be termed a covenant. "Yahweh turned toward them, because of his covenant with Abraham, Isaac, and Jacob" (2 Kings 13:23; see also Ps. 105:8f., 42).[48]

SUMMARY

Before we summarize, it must be stressed once more that the present study is only partial. It needs to be expanded in three directions. (a) The study of the groups of passages in which the individual promises appear should be placed on a more secure foundation by exegesis of the individual passages in their

---

48. A detailed discussion of "covenant promise" and covenant formula appears in A. Jepsen, "Berith," in *Verbannung und Heimkehr*, Festschrift W. Rudolph (Tübingen: Mohr, 1961), pp. 171–72.

contexts.[49] (b) The texts in which several promises are combined should be studied independently and comparatively. And finally, (c) the later history of the individual promises should be studied. Our summary must be restricted to the partial study offered here.

We have seen that the promises have several features in common, but that each of the promises was once independent, and therefore each must be studied by itself. This casts doubt on any summary judgments concerning the promises, their function, their origin, and their history that have not inquired first into the individual promises.

The history of tradition of the promises extends from the patriarchal period to the late period of Israel. The portion still accessible to us differs from promise to promise. It is impossible to say of the promises as a whole that they are very early or that they are very late.

Of two of the promises that have been preserved and one that can only be inferred, it can be said with great probability that they originated in the patriarchal period itself: the promise of a son, the promise of God's aid and presence during a journey, and the promise of new territory (suggested in 12:1-3). The other promises function to link the patriarchal period with the history of the nation, and came into being after the settlement.

Some or all of the later promises represent transformations of earlier rhetorical forms into promises. The promise of the land is based on a formula of conveyancing; the promises of blessing and increase are based on idioms associated with the act of blessing, especially marriage blessing in the case of the promise of increase. The promise "I will be your God" (only in P) may be based on an expression used in oaths, transformed into a promise by P.

---

49. Hoftijzer takes the first steps in this direction.

IV

The Theological Significance of the Promises

The theological significance of the two groups distinguished above must be assessed differently. In the case of the second group, the significance lies on the plane of conscious theological reflection. It is most clearly recognizable in its early stage in Genesis 12:1–3, in its late stage in Genesis 17. Here the promises are viewed from the perspective of Israel *after* its encounter with Yahweh as the God who delivers (exodus tradition). They have the function of bringing coherence into the history of God with his people. The promises given to the fathers provide assurance that the God who promised in the past and fulfilled his promises of the land and of increase will remain faithful to his word, that one can rely for the future on the words and actions of this God. This assurance makes it possible to look back and see Israel's history as a coherent whole and to look forward trusting in God's future actions.

In the first group, the significance lies on the plane of pretheological and prehistorical talk of God, belonging to the period *before* Israel's encounter with Yahweh at the exodus and at Sinai. These promises are a component of the patriarchal religion even before any contact with the history and religion of Israel. These promises go back to traditional experiences of the patriarchs Abraham, Isaac, and Jacob in the context of their nomadic way of life. Here they had the function of attesting to the earliest association we can discover between what a god says (promise) and what he does (fulfillment). They were preserved because deliverance from deadly danger or preservation through mortal peril was experienced as a relationship giving meaning to life. The experience of deliverance or preservation was experienced in

162

relationship to God, as fulfillment of his word. In these promises is revealed the most important analogy between the religion of Israel and the religion of the fathers, and it is understandable that the patriarchal tradition became a component of the tradition of Israel.[50]

50. The theological significance of the promises could only be suggested here; it demands further elaboration in the context of each passage.

PART C

The Significance of the Ugaritic Texts for the Patriarchal Narratives*

*This study of the Ugaritic texts was based on the translation of J. Aistleitner (*Die mythologischen und kultischen Texte aus Ras Schamra*, Bibliotheca orientalis hungarica 8 [Budapest: Akademiai Kiadó, ²1964]); I am well aware of the shortcomings of this work. All textual quotations are based on this translation. Following Aistleitner, all the Ugaritic texts are cited according to the system proposed by O. Eissfeldt ("Bestand und Benennung der Ras-Schamra-Texte" in his *Kleine Schriften, II* [Tübingen: Mohr, 1963], pp. 330–55). For further orientation, the sigla used by Gordon and Herdner in their publications are added in parentheses (C. H. Gordon, *Ugaritic Textbook* [=Go.], Analecta Orientalia 38 [Rome: Pontificio Instituto Biblico, 1965]; A. Herdner, *Corpus des Tablettes en Cunéiformes Alphabétiques découvertes à Ras Shamra-Ugarit de 1929 à 1939* [=CTA], Mission de Ras Shamra 10 [Paris: Imprimerie Nationale, 1963]). Of the monographs devoted to Ugaritic texts, we cite J. Gray, *The KRT Text in the Literature of Ras Shamra*, Documenta et Monumenta Orientis Antiqui 5, 2d ed. (Leiden: Brill, 1964). For the Aqht text, there is only the somewhat dated version of P. Fronzaroli, *Leggenda di Aqhat*, Il Melagrano 136/37 (Florence, 1955). For the NK text, see W. Herrmann, *Yarih und Nikkal und der Preis der Kutarāt-Göttinen*, Beihefte zur Zeitschrift für die alttestamentliche Wissenschaft 106 (Berlin: Töpelmann, 1968). On the SS text, see P. Xella, *Il Mito di ŠḪR e ŠLM*, Studi Semitici 44 (Roma: Instituto di Studi del Vicino Oriente, 1973).

The notes in this section were provided by K. Günther of the Center for Ugaritic Studies in Heidelberg.

I

Introduction:
The Nature of the Aqht
and Krt Texts

From the very outset, the major Ugaritic literary texts have been divided into two groups. The difference was noted particularly by Eissfeldt in "Mythus und Sage in den Ras-Schamra-Texten" (*Kleine Schriften, II* [Tübingen: Mohr, 1963], pp. 489–501). "It is of great importance to keep firmly in view the difference between the epics just mentioned on the one hand and the narratives of Keret and Dan'el on the other" (p. 495). He terms the Krt and Aqht texts sagas, the BAB texts myths (pp. 496, 498).

In a paper delivered at the 16th German Congress of Orientalists at Heidelberg in 1965 (reprinted in *Zeitschrift für Assyriologie*, NF 24 [1967]: 211–21), K. Koch examined "the promise of a son to the Ugaritic Daniel." A detailed study of the "twelve duties of the royal son" revealed a surprising situation: "Their substance is remarkable. No mention of aid in giving counsel, judging, or governing, no mention of support in war or commerce! There is no trace at all of what we would consider the duties of a royal son" (p. 217). He concludes, "All this suggests that we have found here a figure belonging to an earlier religious stage, brought at one time to Ugarit as a nomadic clan religion by a ruling class just settling down. The similarities to the much discussed 'God of the fathers' of the Old Testament patriarchal sagas . . . is immediately obvious" (p. 218).

Both the observation and the conclusion appear correct to me. I would therefore like to raise the question whether the Ugaritic texts do not provide a much broader base for this conclusion, so that the conclusion of close resemblance to the religion of the patriarchs could carry substantially more weight. Continuing in the direction of Koch's observation, I propose the thesis that in the Aqht and Krt texts (as well as the NK and SS texts) an earlier stratum is recognizable, which belongs to an "earlier religious stage" (Koch) and contains a whole series of motifs and motif sequences that have analogues in the patriarchal history of Genesis 12–50. This thesis assumes my determination that the major group of narratives in Genesis 12–50 are family narratives (see above, pp. 1–29).

We are therefore dealing not only and not primarily with individual, isolated motifs occurring here and there, but with a comparable way of life appearing in the texts, having comparable narratives and a comparable relationship to God.

The approach attempted here differs from that of A. Alt, "The God of the Fathers," in his *Essays on Old Testament History and Religion* (Oxford: Blackwell, 1966), pages 1–77, and that of F. M. Cross, *Canaanite Myth and Hebrew Epic* (Cambridge: Harvard University Press, 1973), in that it does not concentrate on the terms for deities in determining the comparable text material, but sees the material in the narratives that relate what takes place between God (or the gods) and man. Since, however, these events always take place within the nexus of human society, the comparative forms of this society must also be studied.

II

Family Motifs in the Ugaritic Texts

The earlier religious stage that Koch hypothesizes behind a group of the Ugaritic texts he terms a "nomadic clan religion." But is what he observed really typically nomadic? It will be seen that the Ugaritic texts no longer exhibit clear features of a nomadic religion, but they do contain a whole series of what are clearly elements of a "clan religion." This is easy to explain. The specifically nomadic features were gradually dropped after settlement, since for the inhabitants of Ugarit they lay in the remote past. But the features of a family religion were preserved long and tenaciously, because the family structures long maintained their determinative significance. This accounts for one aspect of the difference between the two groups of Ugaritic texts: the BAB texts are largely determined by the motifs of fertility and politics, albeit transposed to the mythological realm; the Krt and Aqht texts are largely determined by family motifs. The former could therefore not have come into being until the settled period with its urban civilization; the latter can have roots going back to the period of incipient settlement.

This conclusion puts comparison of this latter group with the patriarchal stories of the Old Testament on a firm footing. So many familial features appear in both because both are set against the background of a group having familiar structure that has just entered the region. At the same time, however, we note the difference that must always be kept in mind: the patriarchal stories of Genesis are much closer to the nomadic way of life; the Ugaritic texts received their form in a highly developed urban civilization in which all the nomadic features had already been lost. The familial structures still dominate the narrative, but they are overlaid by a mythological presentation of the action and by the features of sacral kingship. This agrees precisely with the observations of Koch. The difference is illustrated, for example, by the fact that the Ugaritic texts preserve no trace of anything like a promise of the land, while the promise of a son plays an important role.

THE VALUE OF THE FAMILY MOTIFS

The parallels exhibited below are not significant apart from the contexts in which they appear. In the patriarchal stories, the context is the small group of nomadic herdsmen, with familial structure, before their transition to settled agriculture. In Aqht and Krt, it is, on the surface, an urban milieu in which the primary figure is the king and what takes place is a transaction between gods and men. Beneath this surface, however, is revealed the milieu of an agricultural village, as familial in structure as the form of society depicted in the patriarchal stories, where the important events take place within the life of the family. This appears in the catalog of filial obligations,[1] in which there is nothing to suggest a royal son and his royal office (Koch); it appears also in a scene in Aqht/I D 47–60:[2] Dn il gives his daughter Pgt the job of saddling his ass; Pgt, crying, obeys and then helps her father mount the ass. In Aqht/II D V,[3] when the "skillful one" approaches, Dn il gives orders to prepare a meal and his wife carries out the orders. Both scenes are inconceivable at a royal court. It is inconceivable for a king's daughter to saddle an ass for the king and help her father mount; it is inconceivable for the king to order his wife to prepare a meal for a guest and then for the queen herself to prepare the meal. The situation, however, is precisely analogous to Genesis 18, where the messengers come to Abraham and he gives his wife Sarah an order: "And Abraham hastened into the tent to Sarah and said, 'Make ready quickly three measures of fine meal, knead it, and make cakes.' " In these three scenes, as well as others, there is a striking total absence of the servants who form a necessary part of a royal court. This is in line with the observation that in Aqht and Krt specifically political events fade into the background, while family events predominate. The dramatis personae in both texts play

1. II D I 26–34 (Go. 2 Aqht I 26–34; CTA 17 Col. I 26–34) with the parallels II D I 43ff. (Go. 2 Aqht I 43ff.; CTA 17 col. I 43ff.), II D II 1–8 (Go. 2 Aqht II 1–8; CTA 17 col. II 1–8), II D II 14–23 (Go. 2 Aqht II 14–23; CTA 17 col. II 14–23).
2. I D 47–60 (Go. 1 Aqht 47–60; CTA 19 col. I–II 47–60).
3. II D V 13–21 (Go. 2 Aqht V 13–21; CTA 17 col. V 13–21), II D V 21–25 (Go. 2 Aqht V 21–25; CTA 17 col. V 21–25), II D V 28–31 (Go. 2 Aqht V 28–31; CTA 17 col. V 28–31).

the role of family members; they are designated by this role, and the context of their role is family life. Often the family with all its members is mentioned explicitly, as in NK 33–37:[4] father, mother, brothers, and sisters examining the wedding presents; in SS: husband, wife, and wife's handmaid (husband's concubine); in Aqht: father, wife, son, and daughter. Even a flock of eagles is represented as a family: children, father, and mother.[5]

BIRTH AND CHILDHOOD

The chain of events from childlessness through the promise of a son to the birth of the son constitutes—albeit in very different ways—the beginning of both the Aqht and the Krt texts. The beginning of the Nkl text (4–5)[6] deals with conception and birth; SS deals with childlessness (8), conception (30–50), and birth (51–52).[7] Thus it appears that this is the most frequently encountered motif sequence in this group of texts. Of course it is true that the birth of an heir to the throne is an important theme (as noted by Koch, p. 212); but in all these passages, the birth of the son is depicted in a familial rather than dynastic context. In Aqht,[8] when Dn il hopes that his son will harvest the grain, he is thinking of a peasant boy, not a crown prince.

In the story of Abraham, the promise and birth of a son are something like a leitmotif, introduced with the statement that Sarah was childless (11:30) and concluding with the birth of Isaac in Genesis 21. In both the Ugaritic and the Abraham narratives, the promise and birth of a child constitute a determinative narrative motif. The other components of the motif:

---

4. NK 33–37 (Go. 77 33–37; CTA 24 33–37).
5. I D 121, 135 (Go. 1 Aqht 121, 135; CTA 19 col. III 121, 135).
6. NK 4 + 5 (Go. 77 4 + 5; CTA 24 4 + 5).
7. SS 8, 30–50, 51 + 52 (Go. 52 8, 30–50, 51 + 52; CTA 23 8, 30–50, 51 + 52).
8. I D 66–67 (Go. 1 Aqht 66–67; CTA 19 col. II 66–67).

CHILDLESSNESS, MOURNING AND LAMENT OF
THE CHILDLESS FATHER, WISH FOR CHILDREN,
PRAYER FOR A CHILD

Aqht:[9]

1–16. Dn il mourns seven days

17. In response, Baal comes and inquires

18–23. Baal's words: Dn il mourns because he has no son

24–26. Baal's request that El bless Dn il so that he may have a child (repeated in 35–38)

Krt:[10]

7–21. News of the death of Krt's seven wives

22–34. Lament and mourning of Krt

53–58. Krt's answer: I would like children, many descendants!

SS 8. Mt sits with the rod of sterility and childlessness[11]

In all three texts, the situation of childlessness is the point of departure; in Aqht and Krt, this situation is presented by the mourning of the childless man (only suggested in SS 8), expressed in lament and the wish for children or in the request for a son (Aqht/II D I 24–26), placed in the mouth of Baal as intercessor for Dn il.

In the Abraham cycle, the chain of events begins with the barrenness of Sarah (11:30); the lament of the childless man (15:2, 3; two variants) precedes the promise of a son (15:4). It is noteworthy that in the Old Testament the lament of the childless mother appears more often than that of the childless father (1 Sam. 1; Ps. 113:9); this observation is certainly rooted in different social conditions. The motif of the childless woman, with the suggestion of a lament, appears once more in Genesis 25:19–23; here, too, the lament is followed by turning to God (see also 30:31; 31:1–2; Judg. 13:2–3).

9. II D I 1ff. (Go. 2 Aqht I 1ff.; CTA 17 col. I 1ff.).
10. I K 7ff. (Go. Krt 7ff.; CTA 14 col. I 7ff.).
11. See note 7.

THE PROMISE OF A SON

Aqht:

II D I 39–44.[12] Command to Dn il to beget a son

    II D II 9.[13] Promise of a son (?; text corrupt)

        10–15. Dn il's reaction; he rejoices: "A son will be born to me!"

Krt:[14]

I K   59–153. El's promise discourse, with detailed instructions on how to win a wife

    154–155. Conclusion: it was a dream

    156–306. Performance of what was commanded in the dream

Krt:

III K II 1–10.[15] (fragmentary) The gods come to Krt's house to celebrate his wedding

    11–16. Baal calls on El to bless Krt

    17–28. El's blessing of Krt (continued in III K III 1–16)

        17–20. El takes a goblet and blesses Krt

        21–24. Your wife will bear you 7 sons and 8 daughters

        25–28. List of the sons (?)

III K III 2–4.[16] Krt will be exalted amidst the mighty of the land

    5–12. List of daughters

    13–15. Repetition of 2–4

    16. The youngest of them I appoint as firstborn

    17–19. The gods depart with blessings

    20–24. The promised sons and daughters are born

12. II D I 39–42, 43ff. (Go. 2 Aqht I 39–42, 43ff.; CTA 17 col. I 39–42, 43ff.).

13. II D II 9ff. (Go. 2 Aqht II 9ff.; CTA 17 col. II 9ff.).

14. I K 59ff. (Go. Krt 59ff.; CTA 14 col. II 59ff.).

15. III K II 1ff. (Go. 128 II 1ff.; CTA 15 col. II 1ff.).

16. III K III 2ff. (Go. 128 III 2ff.; CTA 15 col. III 2ff.).

Concerning the beginning of both texts, Koch says, "Each time the alleviation of the distress is announced through a vision, which then issues in the promise of a son" (p. 211). But the two texts are really not so similar; Koch unfortunately does not go into the wording of the promise. There is a kind of limited parallelism between Aqht/II D I and II[17] and Krt/I K,[18] but a totally different event is depicted in Krt/III K II and III.[19] Here we hit upon the difference, extremely important for the patriarchal history, between the promise of a son and the promise of increase. Only the promise of a son is an alleviation of distress, preceded by a description of the distress and a lament; the promise of many sons and daughters (III K II—III), however, has its setting in the wedding celebration and is a marriage blessing, as this text clearly shows. If it is linked here with the promise of a son, alleviating a distress, this combination clearly illustrates a very early association of the two motifs such as we also find in the Old Testament, above all in Genesis 15:1–6. The text likewise shows as clearly as anyone could want that the promise of increase, that is, the promise of many children, is part of the blessing ritual and is thus distinct from the alleviation of distress. The distinction appears even more clearly in comparison with Aqht, where we find only the promise of a son.

In the patriarchal narratives, 18:1–16 is a narrative of the promise of a son; 16:11 is another, in a different context. Both texts are family narrative. We also find the promise of a son in true promise narratives in 15:4 and 17:15–19 (P). In 15:2 and 3, as in Krt, the promise is preceded by the lament of the childless father. The fulfillment of the promise given in 18:1–16 is narrated in 21:1–3. The promise of a son also appears elsewhere in the Old Testament as a narrative motif, for example, at Judges 13; 1 Samuel 1; 2 Kings 4:8–17. In all these passages but Genesis 15 and 17, the motif of the promise of a son occurs in isolation.

17. See notes 12 and 13.
18. See note 14.
19. See notes 15 and 16.

In the promise narratives Genesis 15 and 17, the promise of a son is linked with the promise of increase; 16:10–12 illustrates an earlier stage, with the promise of a son and the promise of increase in parataxis. It can be seen that the linkage of the two took place gradually. The distinction can still be observed in Krt: in I K 57–58, Krt wishes for many descendants; in the brief repetition 152–153, however, the promise of a son occurs alone.

The Report of the Promise's Fulfillment

In Aqht, II D II 43–46[20] depicts Dn il waiting in suspense for the birth of his child; then the text breaks off. Undoubtedly the gap included a report of the birth of the son, who is already able to draw a bow in II D VI.[21] In Krt, III K III 20–24[22] reports that the promised sons and daughters are born.

In the Old Testament narratives of the promise of a child outside of Genesis (for example, 1 Sam. 1:19–20; Judg. 13:24), the birth of the promised child is the climax of the narrative. The birth of the son promised to Abraham is not recounted in chapter 18, but only in 21:1–3. This separation is determined by the composition of the Abraham narrative; in an early form of the narrative, the two went together.

The Report of the Birth to the Father

This motif is developed in SS 51–65[23] (obscure in many passages).

51–52. The women conceive and bear Šḥr and Šlm
52–54. El receives news of the birth of his sons and offers sacrifice
55–60. Repetition
61–64. The children suckled at their mothers' breasts
64–65. The father's joy; he commands sacrifice

20. II D II 43–46 (Go. 2 Aqht II 43–46; CTA 17 col. II 43–46).
21. II D VI (Go. 2 Aqht VI; CTA 17 col. VI).
22. III K III 20–24 (Go. 128 III 20–24; CTA 15 col. III 20–24).
23. SS 52 + 53, 59 + 60 (Go. 52   52 + 53, 59 + 60; CTA 23, 52 + 53, 59 + 60).

This motif does not appear in the patriarchal stories, but the same event is probably reflected in Jeremiah 20:14–18, where Jeremiah curses the day of his birth: "Cursed be the man who brought the news to my father, 'A son is born to you,' making him very glad" (see also Job 3:3).

THE COMBINATION OF PROMISES

The promise of increase, which in Krt predominates over the promise of a son, can be linked with other promises, as in Krt/ III K III 2–3.[24] "Greatly exalted will be Krt amidst the mighty of the land." This is analogous to the promise in Genesis 12:2. "I will make your name great," which is also associated with the promise of increase. This correspondence is important because it shows that the promise of greatness or a great name is an extension of the promise of increase.

THE NAMING OF THE CHILD

Naming can also appear in this context, as the Krt text shows; it might be expected in the context of the report of a birth. The name of the child can also be given at the time of the promise. A statement can also be made about the child's destiny, either at the time of the promise or at the time of birth. Such statements appear frequently in the Old Testament, especially in the patriarchal stories. Here, too, we find a parallel in the Ugaritic texts: in III K III, after the promise of the birth of the daughters in 16,[25] we read, "The youngest of them I appoint as first-born." The same is said of the youngest son in Genesis 25:23 and in 37ff. A statement like this shows once more that the milieu of this text is that of the family.

The Ugaritic texts have more to say about childhood than the texts of the patriarchal history. It is noteworthy that the few such passages in the patriarchal stories, such as Genesis 21 and 22, usually speak of danger to the child, whereas the Ugaritic texts

24. See note 16.
25. III K III 16 (Go. 128 III 16; CTA 15 col. III 16).

speak primarily of the children's happiness and the joy they occasion. This frequently recurring motif points once again to the familial milieu.

We are told how the son grows up,[26] how the children are suckled,[27] what the duties of the son are (in the catalog, four times repeated, of filial duties, found first in II D I 27–34),[28] how the children play,[29] what the father gives his son (a conflict motif, as in Genesis 37),[30] how the son is endangered and dies, how he is mourned and lamented.

The individual daughters are listed by name;[31] the youngest of them is declared the firstborn.[32] The promise of daughters has its locus only in the marriage blessing, not in the distress of childlessness. The duties of a daughter are described in I D 47–66:[33] Dn il orders his daughter to saddle his ass; the daughter does so and helps her father mount. The daughter sets out to avenge her slain brother.[34]

MARRIAGE AND PROCREATION

Courtship and marriage are turning points and vital events in the life of the family. It is therefore not surprising that they, too, appear as narrative motifs in the patriarchal stories as well as in the Ugaritic texts. Genesis 24 tells how Isaac chooses Rebecca for his bride; all the details of a courtship are recounted in NK 16–37.[35] A typical difference appears when the first part of the Krt text tells how a bride was won through a military campaign, whereas Genesis 29–31 tells how a bride was won through hired

26. NK 6–15 (Go. 77 6–15; CTA 24 6–15).
27. SS 61–64 (Go. 52 61–64; CTA 23 61–64).
28. See note 1.
29. SS 66–76 (Go. 52 66–76; CTA 24 66–76).
30. II D V 34–38 (Go. 2 Aqht V 34–38; CTA 17 col. V 34–38).
31. III K III 5–12 (Go. 128 III 5–12; CTA 15 col. III 5–12).
32. See note 25.
33. See note 2.
34. I D 190–224 (Go. 1 Aqht 190–224; CTA 19 col. IV 190–224).
35. NK 16–37 (Go. 77 16–37; CTA 24 16–37).

labor. Despite the difference, however, even in Krt the familial aspect of the event is emphasized more than the political.

A wedding celebration with its accompanying blessing is depicted in detail in Krt/III K II and III;[36] no such description appears in the patriarchal history.

The begetting of a son is depicted in NK 4–15[37] in a strangely ritualized manner; the child to be born is entrusted to the protection of ktrt (goddesses who are especially helpful at childbirth).

DEATH AND BURIAL

The Krt text begins with a "message to Job":[38] a string of disasters has taken the seven wives of Krt, like the sons of Job at the beginning of the Job narrative (1:13–21). It is the same motif and serves in both cases to introduce the narrative.

The message of the death of a child is brought to Aqht[39] as it is to Jacob (Gen. 37:31–35). In both cases, the mourning and lamentation of the father follow. In the Aqht text, the lament of the father, the mourning of the community, the burial of the son, the weeping, and the mourning rites are described in detail.

In the patriarchal stories of Genesis, we read of the death of the father (Jacob: 49:28–33; Joseph: 50:24–26), and also of the death and burial of the wife (Rachel 35:16–20; Sarah: 23 [P]). In all the passages, both in the Old Testament and in the Ugaritic texts, death and burial are depicted as events in the life of the family.[40]

36. See notes 15 and 16.
37. NK 4–15 (Go. 77 4–15; CTA 24 4–15).
38. On the Krt prologue as representing the final stage of redaction, see M. Dietrich and O. Loretz, "Der Prolog des KRT-Epos (CTA 14 I 1–35)," in *Wort und Geschichte* (Festschrift K. Elliger) (Alter Orient und Altes Testament 18; Kevelaer: Butzon & Bercker, 1973), pages 31–36.
39. I D 89–96 (Go. 1 Aqht 89–96; CTA 19 col. II 89–96).
40. I D 106–179 (Go. 1 Aqht 106–179; CTA 19 col. III/IV 106–179).

OTHER FAMILY EVENTS

Additional events of decidedly familial character can be listed. These include the sickness of the father in III K V and especially II K I—II.[41] Even though it is important here that the sick father is the king, familial features retain their significance, for example, the lamentation and comforting of the daughter and son. The patriarchal stories do not contain any detailed account of illness, but the illness of Job and his cure might be cited.

Another element common to the Ugaritic texts and the patriarchal narratives is the blessing on departure (for example, Gen. 24:60) and the blessing of the father on an enterprise of his children (for example, Gen. 28:1–5).[42]

III
Parallels in the Narrative
and Sequence of Events

Literarily, the patriarchal narratives differ from Aqht and Krt primarily in that the latter constitute a self-contained whole that can be termed an epic, while the former are somewhere on the road from individual narratives to larger cohesive structures. But even in the Ugaritic texts it is still sometimes possible to recognize smaller units.

With respect to subject matter, the contingent nature of the narrative is essential to the epic; a unique sequence of events is recounted, with its literary effect due precisely to this uniqueness. This does not mean, however, that individual sections cannot

---

41. II K V (Go. 128 V; CTA 15 col. V); II K I—II (Go. 125; CTA 16 col. I—II).
42. II D V 36ff. (Go. 2 Aqht V 36ff.; CTA 17 col. V 36ff.).

depict something that is far from unique, but rather takes place repeatedly and always in the same way, such as a custom or ritual.

In the patriarchal history we find both. In one group of narratives, the plot is strictly contingent: something occurs that took place only once in just this way in this place and at this time (Gen. 12:10-20; 21:8-21; 25:29-34). There are also narratives based on something that happens repeatedly but has been transformed into a unique event in the narrative. In this group we can include the promise scenes: Genesis 12:1-4; 26:2-5; 15:1-6, 7-21. Then there are narratives that combine a contingent event with a repeated event, such as Genesis 27 and 33. In Genesis 27, the unique event is the deception by which the younger son obtains his father's blessing; but the course of the narrative follows the ritual of blessing in all its elements. In Genesis 33, the unique encounter between the two brothers is described in terms borrowed from court ceremonial. We find similar phenomena in the Ugaritic texts. The first part of the NK text (4-15)[43] is based on a ritual for the benefit of an unborn child; the second part (16-37)[44] is based on a ritualized courtship. The marriage blessing in Krt/III K II and III[45] likewise is undoubtedly based on well-defined custom, as is the blessing of the field in the Aqht text.[46]

The clearest parallel appears in the sequence of events at the beginning of Aqht and Krt: mourning and lamentation (prayer, wish) of the childless father—promise of a son—birth of a child. This same sequence appears in the patriarchal stories in the Abraham cycle; here, however, this sequence of motifs runs through several narratives. In the Old Testament, as in Aqht and Krt, the individual motif of childlessness has the function of introducing the narrative. The fact that the birth of Sarah's child is not related until 21:1-3 is due to a compositional schema that

---

43. See note 37.
44. See note 35.
45. II K II + III (Go. 128 II + III; CTA 15 col. II + III).
46. I D 47-74 (Go. 1 Aqht 47-74; CTA 19 col. I/II 47-74).

was striving to join several very diverse Abraham narratives into a single whole. It is possible that the sequence of motifs observed at the beginning of Aqht and Krt lies behind this schema.

A second sequence of motifs can also be compared, although in this case the parallel is quite remote. The birth of the promised child in Genesis 21 is followed in Genesis 22 by a threat to his life. In Aqht, too, a threat to the life of the promised child follows his birth. The difference is that here the child born to the previously childless father is killed. There is a remote similarity to the conflict in Genesis 22 in that the same god El who promised the child gives his approval to Anat to kill the child.[47] The essential difference is that in Aqht the fate of the child is determined by the mutual hostility of several gods, while in Genesis 22 it is the one God who had promised the child that then demands his sacrifice.

IV

Parallels in the Relationship between Humans and God

THE NATURE OF THE CULT

The type of cult reflected in the Ugaritic texts has an obvious parallel in the cult appearing in the patriarchal stories, namely the absence of any cultic mediator. Wherever we find cultic ceremonies in Genesis 12–50, it is Abraham or Isaac or Jacob himself who carries out the action. This absence of a cultic mediator is something essential in determining the atmosphere of the patriarchal stories: Abraham himself builds an altar, and it is he who calls on the name of Yahweh at this altar. Abraham himself offers

47. III D II 15–19 (Go. 3 Aqht rev. 15–19; CTA 18 col. I 15–19).

sacrifice; Jacob himself calls on his people to put away foreign gods, he himself pours oil on the stone, and so forth.

The same situation obtains in the Ugaritic texts: Dn il performs the ritual of lamentation and then the fertility ritual, the blessing of the dry field (I D). At the conclusion of mourning he offers sacrifice.[48] Krt, too, offers sacrifice himself at the conclusion of mourning,[49] as well as in III K IV, V, VI; II K I—II 38–45.[50]

It is characteristic of this type of cult that the cultic ceremonies are still totally integrated into the life of the group: sacrifices do not have fixed times and places, but arise out of specific situations in family life; for example, the period of mourning for a family member concludes with a sacrifice. The same is true of the cultic ceremonies recounted in Genesis 12—50. They arise out of the particular situation in the narrative. There is a difference, however, in that the narratives in Genesis often deal with the establishment of a cult, which the Ugaritic texts do not.

The common features show that the Ugaritic texts as well as those in Genesis 12—50 illustrate a stage in the cult antedating the public cult, which is characterized by fixed times, fixed places, and cultic mediators. Not until the cult becomes public does worship take on independent existence, distinct from the rest of life; before that it is an integral part of the life of the group.

DIVINE REVELATION

Koch assumes (p. 212) that in both Aqht and Krt we are dealing with a vision in a dream. But only in Krt[51] do we hear specifically of a theophany in a dream: "Then El came down to him in a dream . . ." (I K 36–37). In the patriarchal stories, too,

---

48. I D 180–189 (Go. 1 Aqht 180–189; CTA 19 col. V 180–189).
49. I K 154–171 (Go. Krt 154–171; CTA 14 col. III/IV 154–171).
50. II K I—II 38–45 (Go. 125 38–45; CTA 16 col. I—II 38–45).
51. I K 36–155 (Go. Krt 36–155; CTA 14 col. I/III 36–155).

revelation in a dream plays an important role; that a promise can be given in a dream is shown by Genesis 15; 28; 46:2–4. There is also a parallel in the fact that the dream revelation contains a promise combined with instruction; this instruction always benefits the one to whom it comes. The parallelism even extends as far as the style. The dream vision of Krt concludes in I K 154–155: "It was a dream." The simple early motif of beneficial instruction in a dream has been extended in epic style to constitute a long discourse, which must now be framed with an introduction and conclusion marking the beginning and end of the dream vision. We may compare Genesis 17 (P), where a long promise discourse has replaced a simple promise, with a corresponding framework.

The beginning of Aqht, however, differs significantly. Here we have a different kind of revelation. After a detailed description of Dn il's seven days of mourning, we read (II D 17–18):

Upon his lamentation, Baal approached.
Is it Danil I hear, servant of the prince of the gods?

The god approaches Dn il as he mourns, to ask a question. Such a question also appears in El's address to Krt in I K 37–43, with much more detail. A question of this sort cannot belong originally to a dream revelation;[52] we are dealing with a different notion, analogous to the Aqht passage just mentioned: El visits Krt in his distress and asks why he is mourning. Here we catch a glimpse of a different kind of revelation, familiar from the patriarchal narratives. A god in human form (mal'ak yhwh) visits someone in need and promises alleviation of his distress. The striking parallelism consists in the fact that this type of divine encounter is found in both the Ugaritic texts and in Genesis 16 and 18 in the context of the promise of a son. It is a characteristic stylistic feature of this type of divine encounter that the god

---

52. J. Obermann, *How Daniel Was Blessed with a Son* (New Haven: American Oriental Society, 1946), was probably the first to point out that the beginning of the Aqht text might involve an incubation scene.

or divine messenger approaches the man with a greeting or question, as in Genesis 16:7–8.

In both types of revelation, the promise is given together with an instruction or command. Aqht/II D I 39–44[53] contains the command that Dn il beget a son; it appears in the context of the promise of a son at the beginning of II D II, where the text is very corrupt. The promise of a son is still possibly to be found in 9; in any case, 10–15[54] certainly exhibits Dn il's reaction to the promise. He is overjoyed: "A son will be born to me!"

In Krt, the whole promise discourse of El in I K 59–153[55] consists of detailed instructions on how to win a wife. Then in 156–306[56] we are told how Krt carries out what was commanded in the dream. This combination of promise and instruction is especially typical of the patriarchal stories. It does not appear, to be sure, in the case of the promise of a son, but is found with the promise of the land (Gen. 12:1–3; 13:14; 17), the promise of God's presence (Gen. 28; 46), and elsewhere.

THE PROMISE

In his essay "Der kanaanäische El als Geber der den israelitischen Erzvätern geltenden Nachkommenschafts- und Landbesitzverheissungen" (in his *Kleine Schriften,* V [Tübingen: Mohr, 1973], pp. 50–62), Eissfeldt espoused the thesis that it was El who gave the promises of the land and of many descendants to the patriarchs. His sole interest in this essay is the question of which god originally gave the promise. Thus he overlooks the obvious circumstance that the Ugaritic texts contain nothing corresponding to the promise of the land but do contain the promise of a son and of many descendants. This latter promise, which is the clearest and most important parallel to the patriarchal narratives, he deliberately excludes (p. 55). Here the identification

53. See note 12.
54. See note 13.
55. See note 14.
56. I K 156–306 (Go. 1 Krt 156–306; CTA 14 col. II 156ff.).

of the promise of many descendants with the promise of a son, made by many scholars (for example, M. Noth, A *History of Pentateuchal Traditions* [Englewood Cliffs, N.J.: Prentice-Hall, 1972], pp. 54–55), proves to be a prejudice that conceals the simple facts.

In the promise of a son to a childless father, Aqht and Krt exhibit a clear and important parallel to the patriarchal stories. Comparison of the two texts shows that the promise of a son is distinct in origin from the promise of many descendants, even though the two were associated at an early stage. The locus of the promise of a son is the divine answer to the lament of the childless father, alleviating his distress; the locus of the promise of many descendants is the marriage blessing, in which a relative of the bridegroom or of the bride wishes the couple a multitude of progeny. Both are clearly distinct in the Ugaritic texts, and this fact makes it possible to distinguish the promise of a son from the promise of many descendants in the Old Testament.

This confirms our hypothesis that the promise of a son to a childless father is a necessary and integral part of a narrative. The narrative is determined by the arc of tension that leads from someone's distress to its alleviation. The promise of increase does not have this scope; it originates in the blessing and enters into a narrative when the giving of the blessing is related. This origin accounts for the fixed poetic character of the promise of increase in the Old Testament. As a fixed form deriving from a ritual, the promise of increase is much more easily removed from its original setting and used independently.

If there is no parallel to the promise of the land in the Ugaritic texts, it is because these texts came into being in the midst of a population that had long been settled, for whom the promise of the land had lost all meaning. The same is true of the promise of God's presence or assistance during a journey, which is characteristic of the Jacob/Esau cycle. It is a promise intended for a group in transit, which likewise lost its meaning for the settled population.

V

Concluding Remarks on the Significance of the Comparison

In my article "Sinn und Grenze religionsgeschichtlicher Parallelen" (*Theologische Literaturzeitung* 90 [1965]: 489–96 = my *Forschung am Alten Testament*, Theologische Bücherei 55 [München: Kaiser, 1974], pp. 84–95), I have attempted to show that the traditio-historical context on both sides must be observed when religio-historical comparisons are made. On the basis of this principle, the observation that the promise of a son, familiar from the patriarchal narratives, also appears in the Ugaritic texts (H. Cazelles, "Patriarches," *Dictionnaire de la Bible*, Supplément 7 [1966], pp. 81–156, especially 144–45; K. Koch; and many others) is not sufficient for a well-grounded comparison. We must ask the reason for the parallelism. This question can be answered by saying that we find in a group of the Ugaritic texts the same milieu of familial life as is found in the patriarchal stories. In this milieu, where family events and interest in them is determinative, the promise of a son receives its relevance. The same milieu can be identified with a series of motifs beyond the promise of a son: they are also associated with it, and all center on the foci of birth, marriage, and death (burial). Thus there is revealed for this group of Ugaritic texts a prehistory when the events depicted in them were not yet set at the royal court and did not yet have specifically mythological character as stories involving gods. Only here do the familial features receive the relevance they have in this prehistory; only here do they come clearly to light, so that it is possible, for example, to distinguish the promise of a son from the promise of increase, each having its own particular setting.

I am clearly aware that the sketch outlined here needs to be worked out in thorough detail. I have no specialized knowledge of the Ugaritic texts and will leave this further study to the specialists. Their work will undoubtedly correct many errors. But the milieu shared with the patriarchal narratives, in which events center on the family, appears to me indisputable. This demonstrates that the family narratives in Genesis 12—50 have a parallel that is close in both time and space.

Index of Passages